WE WIN
31 Days Designed to Empower and Encourage Both Pulpit and Pew

Teron V. Gaddis

WE WIN
31 Days Devotional
Small Group Study Guide
Copyright © 2017 by Pastor G Ministries

All Scripture quotations unless otherwise indicated are taken from The Holy Bible, English Standard Version.

Gaddis, Teron V., 1964-
Senior Editor: Ramona Y. Dindy
Edited by: Jamila M. Woodard/James L. Booker Sr.
Cover design: Paula McDade
Author photo: Omar Lampley
First Printing 2017
Printed in the United States of America

Book Dedication

To God be the glory!
Thank you to Almighty God for birthing the
vision within me and giving me the strength to
carry out the vision. Thank you to my team that
has worked hard to make the vision a reality.

I also want to say, "Thank You" to my mother
and father, the late Queen Cleopatra Gaddis and
Levern Gaddis for always believing in me, loving
me and supporting me throughout my ministry.

TABLE OF CONTENTS

PREFACE

God has chosen you to be a WINNER in your Church! God has called you to live a VICTORIOUS life! Are you ready to WIN? Are you ready to step up to the challenge? Do you have what it takes to be a winner, victor and a champion in your personal, financial, marital, emotional and spiritual life? Well, I have good news for you, that is exactly what WE WIN was birthed by God to do in your life.

I grew up in a very athletic family, both my father and mother played basketball growing up. We were not encouraged to play sports growing up. We were, however, encouraged to participate in after school activities. The choice that rose to the top of the list for me and my sibling was sports. My sister gravitated to the arts, modern dance and band, while I and my four brothers played sports at school and in the neighborhood. Whether in school or organized street ball, there were two crucial lessons that were drilled into my head by my coaches. First, the importance of teamwork. Second, was the importance of ownership. Third, was the importance of leadership. Without a team, there was not game. Without ownership, there was no success. Without leadership, there was never victory. Even in Christendom and in God's Church teamwork, ownership and leadership is essential to winning.

WE WIN, moves you from a "me, myself and I" mentality to a Kingdom mindset of "we, us and our." The Apostle Paul in *1 Corinthians 12:12* writes *"For just as the body is one and has many members, and all the members of the body, though many, are one body, so it is with Christ."* The only way we win is to realize we are one. We must develop an "ALL OF US TOGETHER WINS" or "NOBODY WINS" mindset. The Church is the Body of Christ. It is not just a gathering of like-minded people who gather together to develop friendships. The church is the very conveyor of the grace of God to a troubled and needy world.

We WIN encourages you to stop blaming others, whining, being destructive and damaging to the body of Christ by taking ownership of our own moves and motives and becoming better managers of our time, talents and treasures. WE WIN prompts a move from being a stumbling block to becoming a building block. From being a hindrance to becoming a helper. From being an accuser to becoming an answer. *Ephesians 2:19-21* says, *So then you are no longer strangers and aliens, but you are fellow citizens with the saints and members of the household of God, [20] built on the foundation of the apostles and prophets, Christ Jesus himself being the cornerstone, [21] in whom the whole structure, being joined together, grows into a holy temple in the Lord.* The church is quite a unique place where strangers gather together and, over time, form an intimate community. People we previously didn't know, become dear friends who walk with us through whatever life throws at us.

WE WIN challenges you to view the biblical role of Pastoral leadership correctly. During a time where there are so many false and negative representations of the Pastor, through prayer WE WIN encourages us to look at what the Bible says about the Pastor.

WE WIN connects the Word of God with the spiritual weapon of prayer to ensure, encourage, empower and equip a winning philosophy in the life of the individual church member, the entire church membership, along with the Pastor/Pastoral team.

Your victory on this journey is guaranteed. Whether you are new to this thing called prayer or you already have an established prayer life, WE WIN will grow your prayer life.

1. You must be committed.
2. Set aside a regular time daily to read the devotion for the day and pray.
3. Write out your prayers.
   a. The prayer for your Pastor has been included with each day.
   b. There is space provided for you to pray the Word of God over you and your church family.
4. Get an accountability partner.
5. Ask a friend, your prayer group, your ministry group to join you in the journey.

Know that you are not alone in this fight. Trust God and know that you don't fight for victory you fight from victory. The devil is already defeated. Now walk in your victory!

DAILY DEVOTIONALS

DAY 1

Read: I Corinthians 11:1-3.

We live in a world that is seemingly fond of chaos and confusion. And somehow these things have made their way into the Church of God. This is not a new fact. This was also the case when the Apostle Paul wrote in **1 Corinthians 11:1-3** *¹ Be imitators of me, as I am of Christ. ² Now I commend you because you remember me in everything and maintain the traditions even as I delivered them to you. ³ But I want you to understand that the head of every man is Christ, the head of a wife is her husband, and the head of Christ is God.*

Paul starts out with commending the believers at Corinth for following his example and his teaching when he was with them. He commends them for their willingness and obedience to follow God's order and ordinances. He then makes a sharp turn by moving from commending to correcting some of the Christians in the church who were out-of-order. Some had allowed their conduct and behavior to slip back into some of their old customs and some had moved quickly into new worldly practices. Paul charges them quickly and firmly of their need to understand the head of every man is Christ; the head of every woman was man and the head of Christ was God. Please note this passage is not diminishing or dismissing the role of man, woman or Christ but God is a God of order and the necessity on our part to honor such order as an act of worship to Him.

Today, pray your Pastor will surrender to the Headship of God. Pray your Pastor recognizes the proper headship and relationship with God in the local church. God's designed plan is for the Pastor to operate and exercise headship under the authority of Christ. Pray your pastor subjects himself to God. Pray your Pastor will serve, work and function under the authority of the God who called him into the Gospel ministry. Pray your Pastor understands that God has called him into divine partnership and every partnership must have a head and God is the Head.

MY PRAYER:

_____

_____

_____

_____

_____

_____

_____

_____

_____

_____

_____

_____

_____

DAY 2

Read I Corinthians 7:35.

Every year nearly 450,000 people are injured in crashes involving a driver who was distracted in some way and over 330,000 or 78% of these accidents were caused by someone texting while driving. Likewise, in Pastoral ministry distractions have been the cause of many incidences, accidents and collisions. Distractions have been the cause of church splits, church hurts, and church closings. In I Corinthians 7 the Apostle Paul emphasizes living without distractions. While there has been much confusion and discussion on this text about whether to marry or not to be marry, I think if we pull the curtain back far enough we will hear what God's Word is truly saying. *1 Corinthians 7:35 (ESV)* [35] *I say this for your own benefit, not to lay any restraint upon you, but to promote good order and to secure your undivided devotion to the Lord.*

In chapter 7 Paul speaks on the state of singleness and of marriage. The emphasis is not about one being more spiritual than the other; it is about one requiring a greater measure of maturity than the other. When one is single, they can devote their unwavering and undivided attention to the Lord and His Word, His Work and His Will. A married saint would have to consider his or her mate and possibly the children. This leads to divided attention and loyalties, of which both are distractions. In the same way texting and drive is dangerous and devastating, so too is trying to serve God with distractions, undivided devotion and with reservations.

Today, pray your Pastor will not be distracted from the preaching, teaching, praying and discipling of the saints. Pray your Pastor's eyes will be focused and placed firmly on things mandated by God to equip the saints for the work of ministry. Pray your Pastor's eyes are always watching and his heart is always praying for the sheep that are under his care. Pray your Pastor will not be distracted by temptation, trials and the attraction of the world around him. May they always be focused on the moves of the Master.

MY PRAYER:

_____

_____

_____

_____

_____

_____

_____

_____

_____

_____

_____

_____

_____

_____

_____

_____

DAY 3

Read Ephesians 5:1-2.

Have you ever caught a whiff of something and a flurry of vivid memories come flooding back? I do. Mine are often from my childhood. One of those smells or aromas is that of butter cookies. Teresa Porter, who was both my sister and my secretary for nearly 10 years before she went home to be with the Lord a few years ago, was an incredible cook. She loved cooking so much so that she would often watch a cooking show to try new recipes. Many times, during the week she would cook for us. I would leave for a meeting and return to my office to the sweet aroma of some succulent dish she would have made for lunch and of course my favorite was, you guessed it, butter cookies. You know the ones they made in elementary school. As I am writing this I can almost smell them in the air.

That is exactly what the Apostle Paul was sharing in *Ephesians 5:1-2 [1] Therefore be imitators of God, as beloved children. [2] And walk in love, as Christ loved us and gave himself up for us, a fragrant offering and sacrifice to God.* The word, *"therefore,"* in hermeneutics is always important. My college professor taught me years ago that 'whenever you see a *"therefore"* in the Bible, you have to see what it is *'there for!'* This has proved to be true in my nearly 35 years of preaching ministry. *"Therefore"* marks the transition from what is said and what the results or consequences are of what has been said. The *"therefore"* in chapter 5 refers to the *"new life"* to come in chapter 4 which leads to the *"new walk"* in chapter 5.

Paul littered the book of Ephesians with the word "walk". Some six or more times he uses the word "walk" to speak of the conduct of a follower of Christ, specifically how one is to live after giving their life over to God through Jesus Christ and falling in love with Him. Paul wrote to these believers to encourage them to live their lives out loud as they walked in and walked out their love. Our love from God and for God should cause us to respond to His love. Paul compares Jesus' sacrificial death on the cross to the Old Testament "sweet aroma" sacrifices that were presented at the altar of the temple. The idea behind "sweet aroma" or "sweet savor" is simply that as believers we should always remember the sacrifice

What is it about a smell or an aroma that can trigger memories so strong and so real it feels like you have been transported back in time? The concept is known as "odor evoked autobiographical memory" or the Proust phenomenon, named after French writer Marcel Proust. Like the Proust phenomenon, Paul is saying that the fragrant offering and sacrifice of Jesus Christ's death, burial, and resurrection ought to be like a "sweet aroma" or "sweet savor". This aroma should always remind us of this great sacrifice and the love of God. And when we are reminded it should cause the believer to walk in love, just as Christ has loved us and given Himself as an offering and a sacrifice to God.

Today, pray your Pastor will never forget the sweet aroma of Christ's sacrifice, His death, burial and resurrection. Pray your Pastor will always remember the miracle of faith in Jesus Christ that brings about a new life. Pray your Pastor will be transported back in time each time to Calvary in his private time and public proclamation. Pray the cross of Jesus will forever be before your Pastor as a beacon of hope for those who are the least, lost, lonely and left-out.

MY PRAYER:

_____

_____

_____

_____

_____

_____

_____

_____

_____

_____

_____

_____

_____

_____

DAY 4

Read Isaiah 55:3.

I grew up in generation built on the premise if your parents called your name and you heard them, you would immediately stop whatever you were doing and heed to the call. My younger brother, Brent, loved cartoons to the extent he would zone out while watching. Everyone knew if Brent was watching television, he would often become so engrossed that he would get lost in what he was watching and miss the call to dinner or to get ready. His problem was he would get so caught up in what he was watching that he couldn't hear what was being said to him. Likewise, in *Isaiah 55:3*, God invites us to first "hear" and to "heed" and then He promised an "inheritance." ***Incline your ear, and come to me; hear, that your soul may live; and I will make with you an everlasting covenant, my steadfast, sure love for David.*** *"Come to me with your ears wide open. Listen, and you will find life.* **(NLT))** *Pay attention, come close now, listen carefully to my life-giving, life-nourishing words.* **(The Message)** At the time this verse was written, the people were living on and building their lives on things that would never ever satisfy. Things that included cheap counterfeits, sad substitutes, and fake fabrications of the life God was calling them to.

Five times in the first three verses, God calls them to *"come"* to Him. God invites those who work hard to dig wells, care for flocks and herds, plant seeds, and tend to their vineyards, to simply "come" to Him and He will freely give them everything they are working, worrying and weary over. The secret is in the "hearing" and the "coming." If there is a need, a thirst or a desire in your life for something greater, something bigger or if you are just tired of living a mediocre life, hear the Word, the Voice of the Lord and Come, He will give you what you need. All it takes is a positive response. God is calling you. Finally, God promises to *"make an everlasting covenant with you."* A covenant is an agreement God makes with His people. Some covenants are conditional. In this covenant, there are only two requirements "hearing" and "coming." God promises to make an unconditional, everlasting covenant to bless those who will "hear" and those who will "come." In other words, He is promising *"eternal security," "once saved always* saved," or "*eternal life.*" Those who come to God and accept His offer will experience salvation and the promise that their salvation will last for all eternity! This is the great promise of the New Testament! Those who receive Jesus as their Savior never have to fear He will take their salvation away from them.

Today, pray your Pastor will always be in tune to the tone and tenor of God's voice. Pray that hearing from God is the top pursuit, priority and purpose of your Pastor's life. Pray your Pastor will always be watchful of the things that may block him/her from hearing from God. Pray that your Pastor's heart is set to not only hear from God but to heed God's invitation to come find contentment and eternal security. Pray your Pastor will possess eternal life, understand eternal security and claim the everlasting covenant with God, through Jesus Christ.

MY PRAYER:

_____

_____

_____

_____

_____

_____

_____

_____

_____

_____

_____

_____

_____

_____

_____

_____

_____

DAY 5

Read Psalm 139:23.

The verb *"search"* means *"to examine with pain and care."* The Lord has blessed me to travel many miles across the country and a few times outside our borders. One of the things that changed after September 11, 2001 was how we were allowed to move through airports. Tougher restrictions were made as to what passengers could carry on to a commercial airline. Searches were also made stricter because of the threat of another terrorist attack. Not only were bodies and bags searched, the airline wheelchairs were searched, shoes, belts, purses and even electronics devices were even checked and searched. The new procedures were time consuming, pain-staking, and just a down right inconvenience. Nevertheless, it was all for our safety and security. So, I was thankful. In my airport experiences, I have seen passengers, especially when they are late, get downright rude, nasty and mean all because the TSA is following guidelines given to him or her to keep us all safe. As for me, I always tried to be as kind as I could ever be knowing, that if I happened to be late, it was not the TSA worker's fault. The TSA was not there to make my life more difficult. The TSA worker is there to make my life safer by searching everyone. No exceptions.

The truth of this Psalm is there is absolutely nothing that we can hide from God, not one thought, not one action, not one feeling. In no circumstance can we deceive God, escape God, or ignore God, so the Psalmist tells us we might as well surrender to the searching process. Listen to David's request of God, who knows everything. *Psalm 139:23* **says, "Search me, O God, and know my heart! Try me and know my thoughts!"** I love how the Peterson Message translation renders this verse *"Investigate my life, O God, find out everything about me; Cross-examine and test me, get a clear picture of what I'm about."* This should be our prayer each day. Lord search my heart, know my anxieties, my concerns, my struggles, my temptations, my sins and my short-comings, forgive me and lead me in your path. We should ask the Lord to do the examining because by nature we have the tendency to think more highly of ourselves than we ought. We must allow God, the Creator, to examine and search the

25

creation. He knows our hearts and His purpose and plan for our lives. It is best to cooperate with the Word of God as the Spirit of God searches us, speaks to us and stands us up. Here is the wonderful truth about God searching us, He loves us and wants the very best for us.

Today, pray your Pastor will surrender to God's search. Pray your Pastor will understand the wonderful truth that God is searching us because He loves and cares for us. Pray your Pastor will possess a deep spiritual desire for God to reveal what is truly in his heart. Pray your Pastor will welcome the testing and the trying of his heart, faith and trust. Pray that in your Pastor's quiet time that God would correct his heart, and yet, calm his heart and comfort his heart.

MY PRAYER:

_____

_____

_____

_____

_____

_____

_____

_____

_____

_____

_____

_____

_____

_____

_____

_____

_____

DAY 6

Read Psalm 121.

This is one the most beautiful Psalms of the Psalmist. *Psalm 121:1-8 I lift up my eyes to the hills. From where does my help come? [2] My help comes from the LORD, who made heaven and earth. [3] He will not let your foot be moved; he who keeps you will not slumber. [4] Behold, he who keeps Israel will neither slumber nor sleep. [5] The LORD is your keeper; the LORD is your shade on your right hand. [6] The sun shall not strike you by day, nor the moon by night. [7] The LORD will keep you from all evil; he will keep your life. [8] The LORD will keep your going out and your coming in from this time forth and forevermore.* While I know that today we are focusing on verse 3 alone; please forgive me for including the entire text. I just love this Psalm! Psalm 121 is what is called an "antiphonal psalm" that was used by pilgrims as they journeyed to worship celebrations in Jerusalem. It was a sort of "responsorial singing" or in Native or African American cultures the kind of singing known as "call and response." The leader or the first group would open with verses 1-2, and a different leader or different group would answer with verses 3-4. The theme of this song is God protects his people. I do not know a greater song to sing as they made their way through dangerous paths, valleys, mountainous terrain, under the hot sun of the day and the cold chill of the dark night with fierce enemies, both animals and humans, lurking. In this song, the word "keep" is used six times to remind us the sovereign safety of the Shepherd will keep us safe

Our focus verse is Psalm 121: 3 where the Psalmist wrote, *He will not let your foot be moved; he who keeps you will not slumber.* The word translated "move" means "to slip or slide, to stagger, to be shaken." As the people journeyed on their pilgrimage to worship, there were slippery rocks that could cause injury, a break, a fall, and even worse, death on the uneven rocky, hilly and dangerous path. Despite the danger. the Psalmist stresses in verse 2-3, our help came from the Lord who made the heaven and the earth and the same Lord was concerned about our feet and our walk. He will not let our feet be moved and He will keep us. He will keep our walk while He keeps watch. The word "keep" means "to guard and protect." God is guarding and protecting us all day and all night. Even while we sleep, God watches over us because He does not go to sleep. We can rest because He never needs rest.

Today, pray for your Pastor that God will keep his feet from stumbling, allowing your Pastor to stand firm in God's will, way and Word. Pray that God will protect your Pastor from those small things that can cause tripping, slipping and even worse, breaking. Pray your Pastor can stand on the Word of God during a time in Biblical history that so many are standing on uneven rocky, hilly and the dangerous path of unsound doctrine. Pray the Lord will keep watch over your Pastor's walk and over his way. Pray your Pastor will allow the Lord to keep him.

MY PRAYER:

_____

_____

_____

_____

_____

_____

_____

_____

_____

_____

_____

_____

_____

_____

_____

_____

DAY 7

Read Mark 4:15.

Satan is a thief, robber, burglar and a bandit. It is in John's gospel we find Jesus sharing the fourth I AM statement declaring I AM the Good Shepherd. It is with this statement that Jesus sharply contrasts Himself against false shepherds who He describes as thieves and robbers. Listen to what Jesus says in John 10:7-11 *⁷ So Jesus again said to them, "Truly, truly, I say to you, I am the door of the sheep. ⁸ All who came before me are thieves and robbers, but the sheep did not listen to them. ⁹ I am the door. If anyone enters by me, he will be saved and will go in and out and find pasture. ¹⁰ The thief comes only to steal and kill and destroy. I came that they may have life and have it abundantly. ¹¹ I am the good shepherd. The good shepherd lays down his life for the sheep."* Satan is the thief whose ultimate purpose and plan is to destroy.

Mark 4:15 says, ***And these are the ones along the path, where the word is sown: when they hear, Satan immediately comes and takes away the word that is sown in them.*** In the fourth chapter of Mark, Jesus is again teaching, as only He could, in a parable. A parable is a story Jesus would often place alongside his teaching to help people understand its meaning. The definition I heard of a parable early in my ministry and have never forgotten is that a parable is an "earthly story with a heavenly meaning." In this parable Jesus is sharing with His disciples why He was not impressed by the large crowds but only changed lives. The seed, Jesus spoke of, represented God's Word. The sower is the preacher and the different types of soil represents human hearts. The enemy, who I introduced earlier, seeks to steal, kill and destroy the seed to stop its growth. Therefore, we should never diminish, discount or discredit the destructive power of Satan. He is our enemy, our adversary, our antagonist who seeks to weaken us, wreck us, worry us, and wear us all out if we let him. 1 Peter 5:8-11 *8 Be sober minded; be watchful. Your adversary the devil prowls around like a roaring lion, seeking someone to devour. 9 Resist him, firm in your faith, knowing that the same kinds of suffering are being experienced by your brotherhood throughout the world. 10 And after you have suffered a little while, the God of all grace, who has called you to his eternal glory in Christ, will himself restore, confirm, strengthen, and establish you.* [11] *To him be the dominion forever and ever. Amen.*

Today, pray your Pastor will hold on to the Word of God so tight that the enemy cannot snatch the Word out of his hands. Pray your Pastor will understand the only weapon we are given to defend ourselves with is the Sword of the Spirit, which is the Word of God. Pray your Pastor, as God's under-shepherd, will understand the enemy seeks to steal, kill and destroy God's sheep and the Word of God has been given to him to defend the sheep. Pray that, as under-shepherd, your Pastor will understand the Word of God is a sword, but also a rod to correct and a staff to care and comfort.

MY PRAYER:

_____

_____

_____

_____

_____

_____

_____

_____

_____

_____

_____

_____

_____

_____

_____

_____

_____

DAY 8

Read Philippians 4:8.

A Mind Is a Terrible Thing to Waste — you know the phrase, you've heard it before. It is the iconic slogan, dreamt up by the advertising agency Young & Rubicam more than four decades ago. Launched in 1972 to encourage Americans to support the United Negro College Fund, this campaign has helped raise more than $2.2 billion and has helped to graduate more than 350,000 minority students from undergraduate college and beyond. Through the years, the slogan has remained unchanged and has become part of the American vernacular.

The Bible has a unique way of saying "A mind is a terrible thing to waste" by telling us what to focus our minds on. In *Philippians 4:8* we find these words, *Finally, brothers, whatever is true, whatever is honorable, whatever is just, whatever is pure, whatever is lovely, whatever is commendable, if there is any excellence, if there is anything worthy of praise, think about these things.* The mind is the seat of the intellect, the will and the emotions. It is where we think, feel and decide. It is also the place where all conflicts we face in this life begin! You see, the mind is the ultimate battlefield of life. The Lord, the flesh and the devil are all battling for control of our minds. Why does the battle rage there? Because the Bible says, "For as a man thinketh in his heart, so is he…"

The words Paul uses in Philippians 4: 8 are a picture of the Word of God. The Word of God is true. Since the Bible is true, everything it says fits within the categories mentioned by Paul. It is honest (honorable), it is just (right), it is pure (holy, clean), it is lovely (beautiful), it is of a good report (good reputation), it is full of virtue (excellence) and praise (that which tends toward worship).

Today, pray your Pastor will fix his mind on the things of God. Pray God will fill your Pastor's mind with the Word, so there will be no room for evil, no room for worry, no room for fear, no room for vengeance, and no room for confusion and trouble. Pray as your Pastor's mind is filled with Word of God that it will also be led by the Word of God and become a stable mind!

MY PRAYER:

_____

_____

_____

_____

_____

_____

_____

_____

_____

_____

_____

_____

_____

_____

_____

_____

DAY 9

Read Ephesians 5:18.

Dionne Warwick release a song in 1966 entitled, "What the World Needs Now Is Love." Let me ask you a question. What does the Church need now? I believe if there is one thing the church, clergy and congregation need more of, it is the Holy Spirit. We need more of the medicine Paul is prescribing in Ephesians 5 verses 18-21. I want to go on record right here and tell you what the church needs is Him and all that He brings with Him. We need Him and His presence and His power in a desperate way. We should not fear the Spirit of God, but we should welcome Him and create an atmosphere where He feels at home, an atmosphere where He can work unhindered, unimpeded, unobstructed, and unconstrained in the church.

Ephesians 5:18 says, ***And do not get drunk with wine, for that is debauchery, but be filled with the Spirit.*** Here the Apostle Paul is telling the Ephesian believers what the Holy Spirit offers. He offers control, just as alcohol controls the life of an alcoholic, so too, the Holy Spirit should control the life of a follower of Christ. He should control the Christian walk, talk, thoughts, attitudes, actions, and mood. There are a couple of things the Spirit of God offers I want to share with you. The Spirit of God offers completeness. The word "filled" means to "be full to the top, lacking nothing, nothing short of complete." The believer's life ought to be so full of the Spirit that there is no room for anything else. The Spirit of God offers consistency. The verb "filled" is in what is called the "active tense." This means it is to be a constant state of being. In other words, we have been "filled." We are being "filled." And we are commanded to keep being "filled" with the Spirit over and over again.

Today, pray your Pastor be filled with the Spirit of God. Pray your Pastor will operate under the leadership of the Holy Spirit and cooperate with the Holy Spirit. Pray that just as an alcohol controls an alcoholic, the Spirit will control the Pastor. Pray your Pastor will avail his walk, talk, thoughts, attitudes, moves and moods to the leadership and the headship of the Spirit of God. Pray your Pastor has received the filling of the Holy Spirit in the new birth and continues to be filled through studying the Word of God, prayer to God, and communion with God.

MY PRAYER:

_____

_____

_____

_____

_____

_____

_____

_____

_____

_____

_____

_____

_____

_____

DAY 10

Read Proverb 4:26.

The key verse of the fourth chapter of Proverbs is verse 18. *But the path of the righteous is like the light of dawn, which shines brighter and brighter until full day.* This verse gives the image of a new day of possibilities. If we walk in the will, the way and the wisdom of God, our path and our day will get brighter and brighter and there will be no sunset. In Heaven, there will be no night and there will be no need for a sun. God's desire is that, as believers, we should walk in His path. But let me quickly say that walking in God's path will not be smooth sailing or a walk in the park. There will be the temptation to walk behind God, walk before God and even walk away from God.

In verses 20-26, the Father is telling his son that knowing God, leads to trusting God, which results in obeying God. He warns his son to beware of what he allows to enter and exit his ears (v. 20), his heart (v. 23), his mouth (v. 24), his view (v. 25), and his path (v. 26). The lessons taught here are also valuable for us. It reminds us what enters our ears, will eventually enter our hearts, and will ultimately come out of our mouth. And furthermore, if what enters is not the right thing it will then distort our view and values.

Proverbs 4:26-27 says, *²⁶ Ponder the path of your feet; then all your ways will be sure. ²⁷ Do not swerve to the right or to the left; turn your foot away from evil.* The Hebrew word translated "ponder" means "to weigh or to make level." It is related to a word that means "scales." So, what does it mean to ponder? It means to weigh a matter mentally, to consider it carefully, to think about it, to muse over it, and to meditate upon it. In today's world, most of us are too busy with so much noise and activity to stop and think soberly about our lives. Instead of musing, we seek amusements – activities designed to distract us from any real deep contemplation. Instead of self-examination about our lives, we chase more entertainment. Instead of thinking, we drown out internal conversation with the Spirit of God with television, movies, music, drinking, or drugs.

Now that we have discussed what we are pondering let's talk about what we should be pondering. Ask yourself. Are you walking with God and growing in the grace and knowledge of Jesus Christ? Are you bearing much spiritual fruit? Are you forgiving, loving, and serving all others to keep the second commandment? Is your marriage what it should be? Do you have activities in your life that create temptation and lead to sin? Are you single minded for the kingdom of God? Are you walking in the way, will, wisdom and Word of God? If so, God promises to protect your path, direct your path and perfect your path.

Today, pray your Pastor will be sensitive to the correction of God. Pray your Pastor will be open to the same Word that he holds in his hand, studies from, prays with and reads as he stands to preach. Pray your Pastor's toes are stepped on whenever they are tempted to stray from the path set before him. Pray he will ponder his path. Pray your Pastor will grow in the grace and knowledge of Jesus Christ. Pray your Pastor will be forgiving, loving, worshipping, studying, serving and sharing. Pray your Pastor will possess a single-mind for the Kingdom of God. Pray that God will protect, direct and perfect your Pastor's path.

MY PRAYER:

_____

_____

_____

_____

_____

_____

_____

_____

_____

_____

_____

_____

_____

_____

_____

DAY 11

Read Matthew 9:36.

Matthew 9:36 says, *³⁶ When he saw the crowds, he had compassion for them, because they were harassed and helpless, like sheep without a shepherd.* Here Jesus looked upon the multitude that had gathered around Him because of the miracles he had performed. As He looked at the helpless, hopeless, and hurting people, Jesus presented Himself as an expression and demonstration of God's compassion, the kind of compassion all men ought to have for all men.

Jesus *"saw the crowd."* He saw those following Him, those in the villages, in the cities, in the countryside, in the synagogues, on the mountains, by the seashore, by the graveyards, in boats, and in homes and He *"was moved with compassion."* Jesus *"was moved with compassion"* over the physical needs of the men: their thirst, hunger, pain, suffering and their sickness. He *"was moved with compassion"* over the spiritual needs of the men: their lostness, staleness, deadness and sinfulness before God; their emptiness and loneliness and bewilderment; their having no purpose, meaning, or significance in life. He saw them all and He observed and studied them. No one escaped the eye or the heart of Jesus, and as He looked, He saw their departure, depravity, destiny and despair without a shepherd, and Jesus the Good Shepherd *"was moved with compassion"*.

Today, pray your Pastor's arms and heart will be open with the compassion of Jesus Christ. Pray your Pastor will possess the same compassion of Jesus when looking at those that are a part of God's sheepfold and those that have yet to become a part of the flock. Pray your Pastor will see those who are helpless, hopeless, and hurting and long to express and demonstrate Christ-like compassion and care. Pray your Pastor will be moved with compassion over the physical needs of men as well as their spiritual needs. Pray your Pastor will be able to minister, serve, teach, and educate a multi-generational, multi-ethnic and cross-cultural congregation with Godly love and compassion.

MY PRAYER:

_____

_____

_____

_____

_____

_____

_____

_____

_____

_____

_____

_____

_____

_____

_____

_____

DAY 12

Read Ephesian 6:19-20 and Colossians 4:2-4.

I know that it is no surprise to you that that there is a war going on. In Paul's letter to the church in Ephesus, he commands us to put on the whole armor of God. Remember Paul is writing this in prison, under constant supervision. No wonder after being forced to look at soldiers and their armor day after day that the Holy Spirit shares through Paul the importance of the Christian armor. Paul commands us to put on the belt of truth, the breastplate of righteousness, the sandals of the gospel, the shield of faith in God, the helmet of salvation, and the sword of the Spirit which is the Word of God. Then Paul describes the most overlooked weapon in this spiritual war and that is the supernatural provision of the Christian soldier, prayer, a constant spirit of prayer.

While prayer is one of the last pieces of equipment mentioned it is one of the most powerful. The Apostle Paul wrote in *Colossians 4:2-4* these words [2] *"Continue steadfastly in prayer, being watchful in it with thanksgiving. ³ At the same time, pray also for us, that God may open to us a door for the word, to declare the mystery of Christ, on account of which I am in prison— ⁴ that I may make it clear, which is how I ought to speak."* The word "continue" means to be constant, preserving, unwavering and unwearied in prayer. Prayer should be a constant and unbroken fellowship and communion with God. The next word Paul uses regarding prayer is to be "watchful," which means to stay awake, be alert, be sleepless, be active, concentrate and be ready. In prayer, we must fight against distraction, drowsiness, sluggishness, wandering thoughts and useless daydreaming. In other words, powerful and purposeful prayer comes from a heart and mind that has developed the discipline to stay on point. We are encouraged to "continue" and be "watchful" in prayer and then we are told to be watchful with "thanksgiving." Someone wisely said, "If you think about all God has done, you will thank God."

We are to "continue" in prayer, be "watchful" in prayer and be "thankful" in prayer for our Pastors. We are encouraged through Paul's writing here in Colossians to pray for our

Pastor. Remember Paul was in prison. Nevertheless, we should play close attention to his request. He could have asked for a myriad of things but he asked to the saints pray for him. He didn't ask them to pray for his safe and secure release, nor that his life is spared, his charges will be overturned or that his fear of execution would pass. Now, Paul asked the saints in Colossians verse 3: *³"At the same time, pray also for us, that God may open to us a door for the word, to declare the mystery of Christ, on account of which I am in prison— ⁴ that I may make it clear, which is how I ought to speak."* Paul is not asking the saint to pray for legal, monetary, moral, or even material support. He is asking for ministry support.

Today, pray your Pastor will not be ashamed of the gospel, for it is the power of God for salvation to everyone who believes. Pray your Pastor will eagerly share the gospel story every time the opportunity presents itself. Pray doors will swing open for your Pastor to preach and teach all over this community, city and even country. Pray your Pastor will declare the mystery of Christ death, burial and resurrection. Pray your Pastor will accept the assignment of being a prisoner of the gospel story and will see every situation as an opportunity to build the Kingdom. Pray that when God opens preaching and teaching opportunities for your Pastor the Spirit of God will give clarity of speech and thought.

MY PRAYER:

_____

_____

_____

_____

_____

_____

_____

_____

_____

_____

_____

_____

_____

_____

DAY 13

Read Psalm 34:8.

In 1869, a fruit merchant, Joseph Campbell, and an icebox manufacturer, Abraham Anderson, shook hands in Camden, N.J., to form a business that one day became one of the most recognized in the world and a symbol of Americana. "Mm! Mm! Good!" Sound familiar? It ought to! It is the Campbell Soup slogan since the 1930s, when the company entered radio sponsorship.

Early in life I learned that Campbell Soup was "Mm! Mm! Good!" but the older I get and the more I have experienced, I have learned to agree with the psalmist David who challenged God's people in *Psalm 34:8: "Oh, taste and see that the LORD is good!"* It is my prayer and God's desire that at some point in our lives we will discover "The Lord is good! Throughout our life, there are going to be twists and turns, ups and downs, good days and bad days, but at the end of all those life experiences we will discover "The Lord is good!" Everything He permitted, everything He withheld, every difficult moment, every stretching circumstance, God meant for our good.

In Psalm 34:8 David invites us to taste and see that the LORD is good! The sequence of the phrase makes tasting the action and seeing the result. The word "taste" does not imply a sip or a nibble; it implies feeding, devouring, nourishing on, and consuming on the Lord through His Word and experiencing all He has for us. The more time we spend with Him the better He gets. The longer we walk with Him the closer we become. The more we listen to Him the easier it becomes to know Him and to follow Him. Keep chewing on and feasting on every experience, taking in every savory moment. The result will be us knowing Him better, and enjoying Him more.

Today, pray your Pastor will taste and see that the Lord is good and celebrate His goodness. Pray your Pastor will savor every experience knowing the Lord will work everything out for the good of them who love Him. Pray your Pastor will taste, not nibble or sip, but devour every season of ministry knowing that it will be good to the last drop. Pray your Pastor's intimate, quiet time with

God will be sweet and satisfying. Pray your Pastor will grow and mature to the place where he sees God's goodness in every situation and every season.

MY PRAYER:

_____

_____

_____

_____

_____

_____

_____

_____

_____

_____

_____

_____

_____

DAY 14

Read 1Corinthians 3:2.

As I write this day of the devotional, Janice (my wife) is in her twelfth year as owner and operator of a home daycare center and let's just say I have seen my share of new babies grow and mature. Matter of fact, some of her first group of children are either entering or finishing their first year of college. We have fed them bottles of milk, then baby food, then table food. We watched them roll over for the first time, cut their first teeth, crawl, first steps, walk and run. Maturity is just part of life. Never once have we had a child enter the daycare and not grow.

Sadly, as a Pastor I have seen a lack of growth happen far more times than I would like to admit. Where people come to the church and are not growing or maturing as they should. In I Corinthians 3, Paul is painting for us a picture of two kinds of saved people; the mature and the immature; the spiritual and the carnal Christians. *1 Corinthians 3:1-2* says, *"[1] But I, brothers, could not address you as spiritual people, but as people of the flesh, as infants in Christ. [2] I fed you with milk, not solid food, for you were not ready for it. And even now you are not yet ready..."* Just as newborn babies start out on milk and graduate to solid food, so too must baby Christians. The baby starts out with milk, but as the baby grows, the baby's teeth began to grow in, the need for a substance that is more solid.

Over the years I have watched children in the daycare's appetite grow. At first, they can only take in a few ounces every few hours, then more and more, until their appetite become big enough for cereal and milk. As they grow and began to crawl and walk their desire for more food grows from cereal to baby food and milk, three and sometime four times a day until they graduate to table food. Likewise, as a babe in Christ grows from immaturity to maturity their diet must change, as Paul states, from "milk" to "meat." "Milk" represent the easy things of the Word, while "meat" represents the hard doctrines. "Milk" represents what is easy to understand, discover and to take in. "Meat" represents those deep things of God that come through prayer, meditation, pondering, fasting, and developing.

Today, pray your Pastor will continue to grow from milk to meat on God's Word. Pray your Pastor will desire more of God and less of the world. Pray your Pastor graduates from baby food to solid food. Pray your Pastor will grow strong teeth that allows him to tear through the tough things of the Word of God to help the church grow as it should. Pray your Pastor has a steady, balanced diet of the Word of God that he may have what is necessary to help each member of the body grow as they should. Pray your Pastor will grow and develop into becoming more like Jesus Christ as he continues to love, feed and disciple children of God.

MY PRAYER:

_____

_____

_____

_____

_____

_____

_____

_____

_____

_____

_____

_____

_____

DAY 15

Read 2 Timothy 2:15.

Although we live in a day when people do not like to wait, I am a little old school and I still like to be surprised. I have learned to enjoy the anticipation, expectation and excitement of waiting. However, most people do not like waiting. They like to have it now, quick, fast and in a hurry, and even at times that is not fast enough. Whether it's waiting in line, waiting in traffic, waiting for food service, waiting for marriage, waiting on a family, biding our time is more difficult than ever. Fast is not fast enough. It's about fast food, instant this and instant that, microwaves and then everything else.

This is not just a problem for the world but this same attitude has now made its way into the church. We want church to be less than an hour. We want the sermon to be 20-30 minutes. The music is too loud and they sing too long. Even in our personal quiet time, we have drive-time devotionals that we play in our cars on our commute. We read five or ten-minute devotional books written for the man or woman on the go. How about the text message or email devotional that can be read in less than 60 seconds?

We all have heard at least one time in our lives that, "Patience is a **virtue**." Patience is the ability to **wait** for something without getting angry, upset or impatient. Patience is a valuable quality in a person. There are some things worth waiting on, the most important thing being God. Patience will payoff whenever you spend time with the Prince of Peace. God's Word is worthy and worth the time you spend with it.

Paul writes to young Pastor Timothy and encourages him in *2 Timothy 2:15: Do your best to present yourself to God as one approved, a worker who has no need to be ashamed, rightly handling the word of truth.* The King James Version says it this way. ***"Study to shew thyself approved unto God,"*** The word *"study"* has nothing to do with books and teachers. It means "to be diligent, be zealous." "Rightly handling or dividing" means "cutting straight" and can be applied to many different tasks: plowing a straight furrow, cutting a straight board, sewing a straight seam. The Pastor's role and responsibility is to spend enough time with the Word of God that the Word of God becomes to him like the sword is to the soldier, like the seed is to the farmer, like the hammer is to the builder, like flour is to the baker and like wood is to the carpenter. It takes time in study, prayer, reading, learning, seeking and fasting to become one who can teach and explain sound, healthy doctrine and become a workman who need not to be ashamed.

Today, pray your Pastor will sit patiently until he hears from and receives from God the Word for the people of God. Pray your Pastor will not get caught up in this microwave society and will discover the secret of waiting on God. Pray your Pastor will understand that God's thoughts are not like his and God's way are not like his and God's timing is not like his. Pray your Pastor will realize that waiting is to weigh things to discover the deep things. Pray your Pastor will give himself to the diligent and zealous study of God's Word. Pray your Pastor will stay at his desk or stay in his study until he is able to rightly handle, rightly divide and cut straight the Word God has for the people.

MY PRAYER:

_____

_____

_____

_____

_____

_____

_____

_____

_____

_____

_____

_____

_____

_____

DAY 16

Read Isaiah 41:10.

Look with me at *Isaiah 41:10: 10 Fear not, for I am with you; be not dismayed, for I am your God; I will strengthen you, I will help you, I will uphold you with my righteous right hand.* There are two commands in this verse not to fear and five pillars of strength to stand on. The first command, *"Fear not"*, is used seven times in Isaiah chapters 41-44. The second "Fear not" command is "be not dismayed."

Always know that commands are placed in the Bible for a reason. My Sunday school teacher, Sister Ruth Sanders, would always say, "God always replaces a *"do not"* with a *"can do."* If God commands us to do something, there are good reasons to do it and power comes from understanding and believing those reasons.

As the Jewish people faced the challenge of the long journey home and the difficult task of rebuilding, you can only imagine the many thing they were fearful of. However, there was one huge reason for them not to allow fear to enter their heart – The Lord was with them and would give them success after their failure. God said to them, "Fear not, for I am with you. Fear not, for I am your God. Fear not, I will strengthen you. Fear not, I will help you. Fear not, I will uphold you with My righteous right hand." In other words, God reminds His people, and you and I today, that we never have to fear because God is with us. God is our God. God is our strength. God is our help. God will uphold us.

Your Pastor is called to hold on to God's unchanging hand and holy Word in a time when people want to hear from everyone else but God. Pastors have always been under attack from outside the church but now they are being attacked from within the church. Your Pastor is held responsible to speak the truth no matter what it may cause, no matter what the people may do and no matter what they may say. Preaching sound, healthy doctrine in a season in history where people want to only hear motivational, self-help, fairytales of prosperity requires a strong faith, belief and backbone that can only come from the power of the Holy Spirit.

Today, pray your Pastor will find strength to fulfill the call of God that is upon his life. Pray your Pastor will stand against the demands of a secular society that wants to make wrong right and right wrong. Pray your Pastor will weather the attack from outside the church and inside the church. Pray your Pastor will be strengthened through the power of the Holy Spirit to speak truth no matter what it may cause, no matter what they may do to him and no matter what they may say about him. Pray your Pastor will "fear not" and know God is with him, God is his God, God is his strength, God is his help and God will uphold him.

MY PRAYER:

_____

_____

_____

_____

_____

_____

_____

_____

_____

_____

_____

_____

_____

_____

_____

_____

DAY 17

Read Psalm 94:16.

Social justice has been a controversial topic in Christian circles for several decades. Part of the controversy is whether Jesus taught His followers to practice social justice.

The mission and message of Jesus is clearly summarized throughout the pages of the New Testament. Jesus went about giving sight to the blind, liberty to the captives, and deliverance to the oppressed. He did these things
both *spiritually* and *physically*. Sometimes Jesus met people's physical needs before He addressed their spiritual needs. Therefore, to fix what is wrong with the world today His Church should not just look at people's spiritual needs, but also their mental, emotional, psychological, and physical needs as well.

In *Psalm 94:16* the psalmist poses two very important questions, *"Who rises up for me against the wicked? Who stands up for me against evildoers?"* The setting for these questions was during a time of National calamity. These two questions ought to be shouted from the places of worship all around this country right now. As protesters and counter-protesters are colliding in hatred and racism. While the church is sitting silent in their holy huddles with their backs turned and their heads in the sand. God is asking *"Who rises up for me against the wicked? Who stands up for me against evildoers?"* We live in a nation where many have turned their back on God, the wicked seems to be prosperous and the godly are perishing, and many people sit down on God and stand up for other irrelevant issues. Serious Bible readers will quickly notice that the question is verse16 is rhetorical and the writer answers the question himself in **Psalm 94:17** "the LORD!" The psalmist was looking around and witnessing the racism, hate, unjust legal system and a society that exploited the lost, the least and the left-out and he responded, *"If the LORD had not been my help, my soul would soon have lived in the land of silence."*

When days become evil and night become dark, God is our refuge, our fortress and our strength but not for us just to sit, soak and sour with this knowledge, but for us to be the salt of the earth and the light of the world.

God is who He is to us so that we can be who we are in the world.

Today, pray your Pastor will stand against the wicked and stand up against evildoers. Pray your Pastor will stand and practice social justice. Pray God will give your Pastor a vision that will address both the spiritual and physical needs of the flock as well as compassionately having outreach programs that will touch the mental, emotional, psychological, and physical needs of the community around the church. Pray your Pastor will be given messages that attack those racial biases in all of us as he stands and give biblical answers to the events and issues that are facing our country. Pray your Pastor will stand firmly and proclaim to the people that God cares, still comforts, and will be our consolation.

MY PRAYER:

_____

_____

_____

_____

_____

_____

_____

_____

_____

_____

_____

_____

_____

_____

DAY 18

Read 2 Timothy 4:2 and Acts 20:28.

Acts 20:28 says: *"Pay careful attention to yourselves and to all the flock, in which the Holy Spirit has made you overseers, to care for the church of God, which he obtained with his own blood."* Paul felt compelled by the Holy Spirit to leave Ephesus knowing he had done his job well and that he had all the people trained and in place who could continue the work to go to Jerusalem. Have you ever felt led by the Lord to do something? If you have, then you know exactly what Paul was feeling! In these verses, the great Apostle speaks to the Ephesian Elders and Overseers that he was leaving in charge and warns them to "Pay close attention to, watch over and guard yourselves and God's people. A shepherd/elder/overseer must be dedicated, determined and steadfast in his watch over God's flock. Whether we realize it or not, our churches are under serious satanic attack. You see, the devil and the world hates what happens when the people of God hear the Word of God and began to live life for God. And the enemy will stop at nothing to destroy this place of worship. We have all seen the enemy use those who are without the church, as well as, those who are within the church to create confusion, conflict and chaos.

Why should the leaders pay close attention, be watchful and guard over the flock of God? First, there is danger in us. We are nothing more than a collection of old sinful sheep who have been saved by grace by the death, burial and resurrection of the Great Shepherd, Jesus, who still struggle and strain with the danger of allowing certain things from our fleshly appetite to cause us to wander and stray. Second, there is the danger around us, "wolves". **Acts 20:29 *says, I know that after my departure fierce wolves will come in among you, not sparing the flock.*** Paul knew that when he left there would be wolves, "false teachers and myth tellers", that would try and capitalize on the young flock. The third and final reason is Paul knew there was danger within us. He makes it clear in verse 28 to not only watch the flock but also yourselves. Verse 30-32 says, *"³⁰ **and from among your own selves will arise men speaking twisted things, to draw away the disciples after them. ³¹ Therefore be alert, remembering that for three years I did not*** *cease night or day to admonish every one with tears. [32] And now I commend you to God and to the word of his grace, which is able to build you up and to give you the inheritance among all those who are sanctified."*

How do we overcome these three dangers that are in us, around us and within us? As believers, we must desire to know the Word of God, to hear the Word, to feed on the Word, meditate on the Word, study the Word and pray the Word if we are ever to going to be able to detect and defeat these religious ravage wolves that are entering our existence through a myriad of ways. We need Pastors, preachers and teachers to sound the alarm, shepherd the flock of God and guard themselves by doing what it says in *2 Timothy 2:15: Do your best to present yourself to God as one approved, a worker who has no need to be ashamed, rightly handling the word of truth;* and *2 Timothy 4:2, preach the word; be ready in season and out of season; reprove, rebuke, and exhort, with complete patience and teaching.*

Today, pray your Pastor will be a watchful shepherd of the flock of God. Pray your Pastor will be a faithful shepherd of the flock of God. Pray that while your Pastor is called to be a shepherd he has faithfully and willfully giving himself to the Great Shepherd Jesus. Pray your Pastor will be guard the flock he has been chosen to oversee. Pray your Pastor will be vigilant and attentive to the needs of the sheep as he preaches and teaches as well as, to be ready to protect the sheep with sword of the Spirit which is the Word of God.

MY PRAYER:

DAY 19

Read Genesis 2:2-3.

According to *James 5:17* Elijah was a man with a nature like ours, chosen by God to challenge the king and Jezebel's 400 prophets of Baal and to challenge the nation to come back to God. On Mount Carmel, he was God's instrument to prove that God was Lord. But after that amazing victory Elijah sank down into the depths of despair, sat down under a juniper tree and asked God to take his life.

This probably surprises many of you that a man of God, like Elijah would become depressed. Longfellow said, "Some must lead and some must follow, but all have feet of clay." We often see Pastors as super men, super saints or incredible Christians, when in reality they are simple men, with the same weakness, worries and wounds as the rest of us. Yes, even God's men become depressed, drained, despondent and discouraged.

1 Kings 19:4-8 shares with us, *⁴ But he himself went a day's journey into the wilderness and came and sat down under a broom tree. And he asked that he might die, saying, "It is enough; now, O LORD, take away my life, for I am no better than my fathers." [5] And he lay down and slept under a broom tree. And behold, an angel touched him and said to him, "Arise and eat." [6] And he looked, and behold, there was at his head a cake baked on hot stones and a jar of water. And he ate and drank and lay down again. [7] And the angel of the LORD came again a second time and touched him and said, "Arise and eat, for the journey is too great for you." [8] And he arose and ate and drank, and went in the strength of that food forty days and forty nights to Horeb, the mount of God.*

I think it is important to note there are two major experiences taking place. One is Elijah standing tall on Mount Carmel and the other is Elijah sinking low under the juniper tree (1 Kings 18-1 Kings 19). In 1 Kings 18, Elijah is at the height of success and in 1 Kings 19, Elijah is in the depths of despair. In 1 Kings 18 he is on the mountain top of victory and in 1 Kings 19 he is in the valley of defeat. In 1 Kings 18 he is elated and in 1 Kings 19 he is deflated. Elijah is not allowed to enjoy and rejoice in the victory of Mount Carmel before he receives a death threat from the queen saying, "You have killed all 400 of my prophets, but by this time tomorrow I am going to do to you what you did to them." And this roller-coaster of emotions has left him tired.

After the threat from the queen, Elijah did what most of us would have done. He ran. He finally stops running and in defeat sat under a juniper tree asking God to accept his resignation. He felt like a failure. He was overwhelmed by the history of his ancestors and said, "God this is impossible, just let me die." Out of sheer physical exhaustion, Elijah passes out fast asleep right there, probably like many of us have done praying through dark nights. He was psychologically wrung out and physically drained. Catch this...The Lord let him sleep. After a time, the Lord sent an angel who prepared a meal for Elijah, awakened him and gave him food to eat and water to drink. Catch this a second time...The Lord let him sleep again. Once more the angel awoke him and fed him in preparation for a journey to Mount Horeb where he could get away from the people and pressures that were troubling him.

Strengthened by the food, Elijah finally reached his destination.

There are three key things that rest does for you.

Rest helps you get refreshed physically and emotionally.
Rest helps you get refocused on the work that lies ahead of you.
Rest helps you get rejuvenated and excited about the work again.

Today, pray your Pastor will get more than a good night sleep. Pray he rests. Pray your Pastor will recognize the signs and signals that his body sends to know when it needs rest. Pray your Pastor is surrounded by those who will be able to see weariness and worry in him and encourages him to rest. Pray your church will put into place regular times for your Pastor to rest so he is refreshed and rejuvenated to continue kingdom business.

MY PRAYER:

_____

_____

_____

_____

_____

_____

_____

_____

_____

_____

_____

_____

_____

_____

_____

_____

DAY 20

Read 1 Corinthians 9:26-27.

If you had to describe your Christian life with an allegory or an image, what would it be? Slug or an ant, a tree or a rock, a slave or an employee or someone who works 16 hours a day, a retired person or a drifter? The apostle Paul often used images in his letters to the church, such as of a soldier, athlete and farmer.

If you attempt to live the Christian life, it will not be long before you realize how difficult that is in our society. By living the Christian life, I mean living a holy life and aggressively seeking to share your faith to make disciples. We have a responsibility to share the truth of the gospel with others, and this is not easy. People living in sin do not want to hear the truth of God's Word.

It is easy to become discouraged in the Christian life. It is easy to become weary, weak, disillusioned, fearful, even shallow in your confidence, because the battle is hard, it is never-ending, and we are human. That is what Paul is writing about when he writes in

1 Corinthians 9:26-27: [26] *So, I do not run aimlessly; I do not box as one beating the air.* [27] *But I discipline my body and keep it under control, lest after preaching to others I myself should be disqualified.* In these verses Paul used the image of an athlete because the Corinthians would be well familiar with the Olympic Games. Chapter 9 is centered around the theme that in order to win we must pay the price. An athlete must be disciplined if he or she is to win the prize. An athlete must train and not just train aimlessly; but train in a specific area according to rules so that he or she is not disqualified.

Paul saw himself as an athlete who was running the race and did not want to lose his reward. An undisciplined athlete would not have the right diet, right exercise regiment, right technique, right rest or the right training. All of which would result in failure to reach the goal, failure to represent citizenship, and even worse risk your being disqualified.

As Pastor, we should have one goal that includes glorifying God, winning the lost for Christ and building up the saints for the work of ministry. To achieve this goal, we must be thankful for the price Jesus Christ paid for us and be willing to come after Him, deny one's self, take up our cross daily and follow Him. **Luke 9:23.**

Today, pray your Pastor will train to keep from running aimlessly and discipline his body, keeping it under control to build strong muscles. Pray your Pastor will set the right goals, train in the right technique and take in the right diet to be spiritually fit. Pray your Pastor will represent the Kingdom of God as a good example to those that are watching. Pray your Pastor will not be successful in leading other to win and risk being disqualified himself. Pray your Pastor will reach the finish line, win the race and receive the reward.

MY PRAYER:

_____

_____

_____

_____

_____

_____

_____

_____

_____

_____

_____

_____

_____

_____

_____

_____

_____

_____

_____

DAY 21

Read Ephesians 6:10-12.

Most Christians have forgotten the Christian life is not a playground, but a battlefield. As a result, very few of the Lord's people are armed, equipped and ready to wage spiritual battle. Whether we ever believe it or not, we are engaged in spiritual warfare. If we are to be successful in our work for the Lord Jesus, then we must be prepared for that battle and be ready to go to war.

In this passage, we are given insight into the battle we are engaged in and into the weapons with which we are to fight this battle. My friends, we are in the fight of our lives! If we are to do what the Scriptures say and *"stand"*, v. 11, 13, 14, then we must know how to prepare ourselves for this battle.

Ephesians 6:10-12 says, [10] Finally, be strong in the Lord and in the strength of his might. [11] Put on the whole armor of God, that you may be able to stand against the schemes of the devil. [12] For we do not wrestle against flesh and blood, but against the rulers, against the authorities, against the cosmic powers over this present darkness, against the spiritual forces of evil in the heavenly places. We have an enemy and his name is the devil, which means "slanderer, accuser." We get our world diabolical from it. His name reveals his character. From the moment, we are introduced to him in the book of Genesis his business has always been the same to steal, kill, and destroy the people of God.

Paul encourages us to be strong in the Lord and in the strength of his might. We are no longer making that our goal, objective and our priority as in past. We have forgotten that our enemy is a shrewd and a spiritual enemy. He is so shrewd that the text says we must put on the whole armor of God to be able to stand against the schemes or wiles or the methods of the devil. In other words, we must be on guard for the craftiness and the trickery of the devil who lies in wait to catch us and capture us as his prey. He is spiritual in that he confuses us and causes us to fight each other, falling out with each other and never throwing one punch at the real spiritual enemy, the devil.

So how do we successfully fight this devil, this evil, shrewd and spiritual enemy? I alluded to the answer earlier. We are to "stand." *[11] Put on the whole armor of God, that you may be able to STAND against the schemes of the devil [13] Therefore take up the whole armor of God, that you may be able to withSTAND in the evil day, and having done all, to STAND firm. [14] STAND therefore, having fastened on the belt of truth, and having put on the breastplate of righteousness,* The Bible makes it clear in these verses that our goal as Christian soldiers is to stand. This word refers to something that is firmly fixed. It speaks of people who do not waiver. If we are to stand in this day of battle then we must, not only, know our enemy, but we must possess energy to stand for the battle, in the battle and through the battle.

Today, pray your Pastor will stand and not retreat in the face of the enemy and the fierceness of the battle. Pray for your Pastor's strength not to waiver, pause or even quit the good fight of faith. Pray your Pastor will put on the whole armor of God that he may be able to stand against the schemes, methods, and wiles of the enemy. Pray that your Pastor is always watchful, aware and vocal about the shrewdness of the enemy in his preaching and teaching.

Pray your Pastor will understand the importance of having a healthy, whole and holy prayer life to not be prey of the enemy.

Pray your Pastor will not be guilty of fighting and falling out with those that are not his enemies but be strong in the Lord and in the strength of His might to fight the devil.

MY PRAYER:

_____

_____

_____

_____

_____

_____

_____

_____

_____

_____

_____

_____

_____

_____

_____

_____

_____

DAY 22

Read Psalm 119:133.

In 1991 Minister Glenn Burleigh penned a song titled, "Order my Steps." The song was sung and recorded at the Gospel Music Workshop of America by the Women's Choir that year and instantly became one of the most popular gospel songs, so much so that it was recorded by several other major artists such as The Mississippi Mass Choir and The Brooklyn Tabernacle Choir. In 1995 the song was nominated for Song of the Year by the Dove Awards. I have often wondered what made the song so popular? The question that came to my mind upon hearing the song was "Did the people really understand what they were singing and what they were asking God to do?" *"Order my steps in your Word dear Lord. Lead me. Guide me every day. Send your anointing Father I pray. Order my steps in your Word."*

Psalm 119, the longest chapter in the Bible, is strictly about God's law. All 176 verses point to one central theme and that is if we want to live a blessed life or a God-honoring life we must keep God's law. How do we keep God's law? We must meditate on it. To meditate on the Word of God goes beyond just reading it and even the simple memorization of Scripture. It means we focus solely on the Word for guidance and direction asking God to give us a heightened understanding and a deeper knowledge so that we are able to live our lives in accordance with that which we were created for. It is only through true understanding of God's Word that this life makes sense. As we grow in our understanding of God's Word, life's pathway lights up. Therefore, the psalmist says, **"Thy Word is a lamp unto my feet and a light unto my path. (*Psalm 119:105*)** It is like the game "Pathfinder" on the Price is Right where in order to win the prize you must make five sequential steps that are the price of the car. When you go the right way the number lights up and you get to move on, but when you go the wrong way it doesn't and you have to back up. In order for the next move in our lives to light up, our steps must be established in the Word of God.

The psalmist begins in verse 1 of Psalm 119 by saying, **"Blessed are those whose way is blameless, who walk in the law of the**

LORD! To "walk" gives the sense of moving along or making one's way. The psalmist is not referring to a perfect life, but one whose life emphasizes integrity and honesty. I wonder how many of us realize that we were *'born in sin and shapen in iniquity'*. *(Psalm 51:5)* No one is exempt. Our natural inclination is to sin and unless we purposely set out to do something different it will have dominion or rule our lives. Therefore, the psalmist prayed, **"Keep steady my steps according to your promise, and let no iniquity get dominion over me."** *(Psalm 119:133)* The King James Version says, *"Order my steps in thy word: and let not any iniquity have dominion over me."* It is not until we come under the saving grace of God that we begin to have power over sin. The psalmist realized not only would there be temptation from within, but there would also be trials from without. And the only way to win in this battle was to seek the Lord and follow His direction. He had to live his life God's way. He could not do it on his own. This prayer showed a deeper understanding that the psalmist had reached. It was not enough to just do good in this life. His life had to follow a pattern following God's Word, His will, and His way. He needed to do what the Word told him to do in all things and do what the Word told him not to do in all things. That was the way to a steady life. To "keep steady" meant to be direct or sure in movement or firm in position. When our lives are being ordered by the Word of God things may come up that tempt to sway us in the wrong direction; but because we have spent time meditating on the Word of God, the Holy Spirit will then bring those words to our remembrance and cause us not to withdraw from our God-given path. It is in the Word of God that we find safety, shelter and security. *(Psalm 91:1-12)*

Today, pray your Pastor's daily prayer will be to have his steps ordered in the Word of God so that sin will have no dominion over him. Pray your Pastor's time will be free to spend time meditating on God's Word not only for preaching and teaching, but also for right living in all areas of his life. Pray your Pastor will never try to walk this path alone. Pray your Pastor will come to a deeper knowledge and understanding of the Word of God so his steps will be sure and firm in position as he lives out his calling God has given him to proclaim the Gospel message to the least, the lost, and the left out. Pray that as your Pastor walks out his journey his moves are established firmly in the Word of God giving him safety and security in his assignment.

MY PRAYER:

_____

_____

_____

_____

_____

_____

_____

_____

_____

_____

_____

_____

_____

DAY 23

Read Proverbs 3:5-7.

We have all been told at one time or another to simply, "trust God." Matter of fact, it is much easier to tell somebody else to trust God than it is for you to trust God yourself.

Why should we trust God? We should trust Him because God has a plan and purpose for us. And being the loving, caring and wise God that He is, He does not leave us to figure out His will, way or His Word on our own. He wants to guide our every step.

In one of the greatest passages in all the Bible, the wisest man who ever lived, gives us some of the greatest advice ever heard. **Proverbs 3:5-6:** *⁵ Trust in the LORD with all your heart, and do not lean on your own understanding. ⁶ In all your ways acknowledge him, and he will make straight your paths.* Now there are two parts to this passage-our part and God's part. Our part is trusting; God's part is guiding.

Trust in the LORD... The word *"trust"* in

Hebrew literally means *"to lie down on, to stretch out on."* Every time I get ready to board a plane and make my way down the loading ramp to the plane and look down to step into the plane, I notice the slight space between the ramp and the entry to the plane. It is at that moment I realize I am no longer in control. I am surrendering my total trust onto the pilot and the crew. I am putting my full weight down. Now the same way I trust the airline pilot and crew is the same way we ought to trust God.

But notice how you are to trust the Lord **with all your heart.** You either trust God totally or as far as God is concerned, you do not trust God at all. You cannot keep one foot on the ramp and the other on the plane and get anywhere in this life. Now there is a reason why God demands total trust, and that is because He deserves nothing less. If you're going to trust in God you must do it without reservation, without hesitation, without equivocation.

We are also told **...and do not lean on your own understanding.** The word **"lean"** literally means *"to support yourself by leaning on something or someone."* Now this does not mean we are to be without understanding. It does not mean we are to put our mind in neutral. But it does mean we are not to make our reasoning, our intelligence, and what we think, the sole guiding principle of what we do.

In all your ways acknowledge him... We are to acknowledge the Lord in all our ways. That means in our financial, social, recreational, vocational, and marital life, we are to acknowledge God.

Here's the shout, if we will do our part, God will do His part which is this: *and he will make straight your paths.* I want to remind you this is not a stand-alone promise, but it is a conditional promise. You will not be controlled by the plan of God, unless you are confident in the power of God and committed to the purpose of God. God keeps His promises when we obey His precepts, because our obedience prepares us to receive and enjoy what He has planned for us.

Today, pray your Pastor will lie down on, stretch out on and put his entire trust in God. Pray your Pastor will learn to totally trust the Lord with all his heart. Pray your Pastor will give God the trust He demands and deserves. Pray your Pastor will trust God without reservation, hesitation and without equivocation. Pray your Pastor will not to make his reasoning, intelligence, or thinking, the sole guiding principle of what he does. Pray your Pastor will acknowledge the Lord in his financial, social, recreational, vocational, and marital life. Pray your Pastor will see God do His part and make straight his paths.

MY PRAYER:

_____

_____

_____

_____

_____

_____

_____

_____

_____

_____

_____

_____

_____

_____

_____

_____

_____

DAY 24

Read Proverbs 27:17.

As a child, I must admit I did not understand everything my mother and father said, did, or required of me. One of the things that would get on my nerves was all the questions I would get thrown at me whenever I would bring up a classmate, potential girlfriend, or a new friend. What's their name? What does their family do? Where do they live? What kind of people are they? What Church do they attend?

I was never allowed to go over a friend's house or even catch a ride with their parents until my parents met their parents. I could never date a young lady until my mother talked with her mother and our first date was always to church. As I grew up and had children of my own, it became clear to me what that line of questioning and cautious behavior was stemming from. As a parent, you want to do all you can to protect your child and prevent any possible problems that could come from the influence of the wrong friend.

Truth is, when we hang around other people we rub off on each other. The question is, are we rubbing off on each other in a good way, or are we rubbing off on each other in a bad way? Are we pulling one another up, or are we pulling one another down? Are we having a positive effect, or are we having a negative effect on the people we meet. We do not have to try consciously to do either. It will just happen.

The world does not care how it rubs off on others - except that human nature wants people to think well of it, even while it is doing evil. But in our Christian fellowship, we have the responsibility before God to *work* to rub off on each other for good. **Proverbs 27:17** says: ***Iron sharpens iron, and one man sharpens another.*** If we are consistently conducting ourselves the right way, it will rub off in the right way. All we have to do is work on ourselves. If we work on ourselves, then our projection of self and the spirit that will go out from us will be right, and we will have the right kind of impact.

God encourages not to isolate or insulate ourselves but to build life-changing, life-long relationships. We are commanded to build biblical communities intentionally through creating friendships and living out the "*one-another's*". We are to be at peace one with another. Love one another. Be devoted to one another. Honor one another. Accept one another. Serve one another. Carry one another's burdens and, one of the most powerful things we can do, pray for one another. Do we realize that when we pray we are in the presence of God and He has the opportunity to rub off on us? It seems so simple that it is almost unbelievable, but it is the truth. Some of His Spirit reaches out and begins to affect us for good. Prayer is a *major* tool in our spiritual development through God's rubbing off on us. All the while this is happening, our minds are being shaped by Him because we are in His presence.

Today, pray your Pastor will understand the importance of having the right friendships. Pray that only positive and productive people will surround your Pastor that will help push forward the passion and purpose God has given him. Pray your Pastor will have an active ministry where he is rubbing off on others and others are rubbing off on him with godly results. Pray your Pastor will be actively creating and living out the "one another's" by being at peace one with another; loving one another; being devoted to one another; honoring one another; accepting one another; serving one another; carrying one another's burdens, and one of the most powerful things he can do is pray for one another.

MY PRAYER:

_____

_____

_____

_____

_____

_____

_____

_____

_____

_____

_____

_____

_____

_____

_____

_____

DAY 25

Read Psalm 91:4-6.

Fear is a common emotion. There are some 500 various forms of phobias identified, that is, things that bring dread or terror into our lives. A few of the top fears are: Glossophobia: the fear of public speaking. Acrophobia: the fear of heights. Aerophobia: the fear of flying. Claustrophobia: the fear of confined spaces. Agoraphobia: the fear of open spaces. Brontophobia: the fear of thunder/lightening. Necrophobia: the fear of death. We might tease our friends for their fear of clowns or mice, but deep down, we all know we have our own fears. It might not be furry creatures that startle us. Instead, we might fear being alone, or losing everything we've worked to gain, or being rejected. Whatever its form, fear is something we've all encountered at some point in our lives.

Scripture has a lot to say about fear. If you were to google the word "fear" you would find several acronyms for fear. For example, fear is "false evidence appearing real; frantic effort avoiding reality; forget everything and run; finding excuses and reasons, or failure expected and received. Yet in the Bible, not all fear is the same. There are two main ways the Word of God explains and expounds on fear. First, there is the fear of God and second there is the fear of everything else.

In *Psalm 91* the psalmist shares this about fear. *⁵You will not fear the terror of the night, nor the arrow that flies by day, ⁶ nor the pestilence that stalks in darkness, nor the destruction that wastes at noonday.* Night is a time of terrors, because it is often a time of fire, storms, tempests, invasion of enemies, murders, thefts, and robberies. The godly man lies down in peace, and sleeps quietly, for he trusts his body, soul, and substance in the hand of God and knows that, *"he who keeps Israel will neither slumber nor sleep"* (**Psalm 121:4**). When it comes to fear, the Bible reminds us to *"fear not, for I am with you; be not dismayed, for I am your God; I will strengthen you, I will help you, I will uphold you with my righteous right hand"* (**Isaiah 41:10**). There is comfort in these words. You do not have to be afraid. These verses encompass the whole of your experience. Night or day, at any point throughout the week, or any season of life, you do not have to be afraid. But why?

We understand **Psalm 91:5-6** by looking at what precedes it in verse 4: *He will cover you with his pinions, and under his wings you will find refuge; his faithfulness is a shield and buckler.* God is a faithful refuge. He is trustworthy. He is righteousness. He always does what he says. But even still, how is he trustworthy for you? How is his faithfulness of benefit for you today? And tomorrow? It is because God is committed to upholding the glory of His name and unceasingly doing what is right.

We should not allow fear to rule over us, the type of fear that grips, paralyzes and controls. I want a fear that turns and runs to God, finding shelter in Him. I want a fear that trusts Him in the midst of storms, and stands in awe of his amazing grace. I want a fear that lets go of everything in my grip and trusts him to be everything I need. I want the right fear, the kind that chases away all other fears. I want the fear of God.

Today, pray your Pastor's eyes, heart, mind and spirit will be opened and enlighten to the living hope through Jesus Christ. Pray your Pastor will be open to the Holy Spirit of God to be taught the deep truth of God. Pray your Pastor will enjoy his faith, be passionate in faith and bear fruit as evident of that faith as he fleshes out his faith. Pray your Pastor will not be guilty of praying and seeking more from God but rather rest in the truth that God has already blessed us in Christ with every spiritual blessing in the heavenly places, grace, strength, light, peace, love and so much more in great abundance in and through Jesus.

MY PRAYER:

_____

_____

_____

_____

_____

_____

_____

_____

_____

_____

_____

_____

_____

_____

_____

_____

DAY 26

Read Ephesians 1:18-19.

In Ephesian 1, Paul has been praising the Ephesians for their faith in Jesus Christ. There was real faith in Jesus' death, burial, resurrection and return to glory. They had received the Gospel by faith, and it had changed their lives and there was spiritual fruit as evidence in their lives. They were guilty of fleshing out their genuine faith and belief.

Having praised the Church at Ephesus for their faith, the Apostle Paul begins to share that they had been on his mind and in his prayer. *[16] I do not cease to give thanks for you, remembering you in my prayers, [17] that the God of our Lord Jesus Christ, the Father of glory, may give you the Spirit of wisdom and of revelation in the knowledge of him...* You see, Paul had taught some deep truth, some light and some heavy, and he wanted them to know he was praying they would be able to grasp what the Lord was speaking through him. Our prayer ought to be Lord open my mind, my heart and spirit that I might receive the truth of your Word. Let's not be guilty of looking for something more when, in fact, God has given us more than enough. Paul was writing to encourage the Ephesians not to waste time looking for things to make them complete but they should grasp the truth that they are perfectly complete already in Jesus Christ. We are often guilty of praying to God who has given and provided for us with a great abundance of blessings and yet still looking for more. We pray for grace, strength, light, peace, love and so much more when all those things have already been given to us. What we really need to understand is what has already been given to us in and through Jesus Christ.

In verse 18, *having the eyes of your hearts enlightened, that you may know what is the hope to which he has called you, what are the riches of his glorious inheritance in the saints...* Paul prays also that the eyes of their heart or the eyes of their understanding might be enlightened. In other words, Paul is praying that God will turn the light on in the hearts of the Ephesians so they can and would be able to comprehend the deep truth of God. Paul wants them to move beyond just feeling and thinking; he wants them to come to a place of understanding.

What does Paul want the Ephesians, as well as you and me, to understand and be enlightened of? *"The hope to which He has called,"* you and me. This refers to the earthly and eternal destiny of the believer. God wants us to understand the hope of election, the hope of predestination, adoption, redemption, forgiveness, wisdom, our inheritance in Jesus, and the sealing work of the Holy Spirit, which are all the things Paul preached to them about in verses 3-14.

Paul wants us to understand the hope that is ours because of this calling. Some callings offer no hope, but the calling we have in Christ assures us of an incredible future. Keep in mind that the word *hope* in the Bible does not mean *"hope so,"* like a child hoping for a new iPhone or iPad for a birthday gift. The word carries with it *"assurance for the future."* When you and I were lost in our sins, we had "no hope," but now that our faith, trust and life are in Jesus we have "living hope."

Today, pray your Pastor's eyes, heart, mind and spirit will be opened and enlightened to the living hope through Jesus Christ. Pray your Pastor will be open to the Holy Spirit of God to be taught the deep truth of God. Pray your Pastor will enjoy his faith, be passionate in faith and bear fruit as evidence of that faith as he fleshes out his faith. Pray your Pastor will not be guilty of praying and seeking more from God but rather rest in the truth God has already blessed us in Christ with every spiritual blessing in the heavenly places, grace, strength, light, peace, love and so much more in great abundance in and through Jesus Christ.

MY PRAYER:

_____

_____

_____

_____

_____

_____

_____

_____

_____

_____

_____

_____

_____

_____

_____

_____

_____

DAY 27

Read 2 Corinthians 12:9-10.

Have you ever been hurt in or by a church?

If so, you are not alone.

I love God's Church. And as a pastor, I have heard many stories from individuals who have found church chaotic, confusing and full of conflict. Now, not every Church hurts people, but all Churches are made up of people who are bound to be wounded at some point. Some people hurt themselves by sins they committed, others are hurt by the sins committed by others and still others are hurt by the failures, fumble and faults of some leader, deacon, preacher or pastor. This reality can cause people to leave church, leave the faith and in worst cases leave God. The good news for the hurting is that God has spoken to your pain in His Word.

Most of the writing in the New Testament especially in the Pauline Epistles address the issues found in the church. Paul addressed these issues after being made aware by new converts upon the establishment of new churches. A very important fact Paul learned that I want to share with you is the perfect Church does not exist and will never exist. I remember older Pastors often saying, "If you find a perfect Church, do not join it because when you do, it would no longer be perfect." There are no perfect churches because there are no perfect people.

So, let us agree on one fact. Church hurt exists. It exists for the pew and for the pulpit. And no amount of time spent reminiscing, rehearsing or remembering how someone hurt us will ever help the healing process. Imagine you were in a horrible accident and had to be transported to the nearest hospital. Would you spend all your time worrying about who hit you or would your first concern be will you live or die?

With physical hurts, we are told by others to go straight to a physician. But whenever the hurt is emotional, psychological or spiritual, we are told to do everything else but go to the Great Physician. When there are accidents in the church that cause injuries, hurts and wounds, we tend to focus more on the one who caused the accident not the Healer. One of the greatest weapons the enemy of the church uses is distraction. Satan knows healing is readily available; however, he does all he can to keep us away and unaware. Satan would have us forget sometimes God uses our brokenness to bless us. He uses our misery to birth ministry in us. He uses our pain to produce passion and purpose. The Apostle Paul, who pleaded with God not once, not twice but three times to remove his affliction, learned this important lesson found in *2 Corinthians 12:9-10*, **But he said to me,** *"My grace is sufficient for you, for my power is made perfect in weakness." Therefore; I will boast all the more gladly of my weaknesses, so that the power of Christ may rest upon me.* [10] *For the sake of Christ, then, I am content with weaknesses, insults, hardships, persecutions, and calamities. For when I am weak, then I am strong.*

Paul learned to quit focusing on the hurt or the handicap and began to focus on the Healer. Sadly, many of us are still parked where the accident happened, bleeding out, with people pleading with us to take our hurt to the Great Physician.

I live in the great state of Oklahoma and one of the things we're known for is tornadoes. I remember one of the worst tornadoes our state experienced was May 3, 1999 when a F5 tornado caused around 1.1 billion dollars in damage. 36 people died in the storm and 8,000 homes were badly damaged or destroyed. The damage was horrific as I walked through those neighborhoods right after that disaster. Families were combing through the rubble with tears flowing. As much as it hurt those effected, as weeks passed, they had to finish cleaning up the debris and begin to rebuild. Those family did not have the luxury to quit and sit on the sideline and shout to God why? They had to pick up the fragments of their lives and rebuild. Whatever hurt we may be dealing with we can't quit. We must place our hearts in the hand of the Great Physician and allow Him to rebuild our lives.

Today, pray your Pastor will allow God to heal the hurts, heartaches and heartbreaks caused by ministry. Pray your Pastor will understand that there are no perfect people and no perfect churches. Pray your Pastor will not rehearse or remain in the season of hurt but will grow in grace, love and understanding. Pray God will protect your Pastor from the trap of the enemy to handcuff, hinder and hold your Pastor in the past pain and that he will allow God to bring about passion and purpose out of the pain.

MY PRAYER:

_____

_____

_____

_____

_____

_____

_____

_____

_____

_____

_____

_____

_____

_____

_____

_____

DAY 28

Read 1 Peter 1:13-16.

Growing up, my family would often remark how much I looked like my dad. I heard it first from those closest to me, my grandparents, mother and siblings. Then I began to hear it at family gatherings from those who only saw me occasionally. Now, that I am over a half a century old, I can be walking in a department store and an older person that knew my dad will stop me and ask me my name and remark about how much I resemble my dad. I have heard it so much I will often respond to my family and close friends, "Who else am I supposed to look like, he was my daddy."

Likewise, as we become a part of God's family, through the wonderful work of Jesus Christ's death, burial and resurrection, we start out as babes in Christ and as we mature those who are eyewitness of our maturity ought to accuse us of looking, acting, talking and walking like our heavenly Father. This is exactly what God wants from us.

Our text puts it very simply. Be holy because I am holy. Holiness is a word that remains a mystery in the minds and hearts of most Christians. We know what the word means by definition, but we have a hard time explaining what holiness looks like. So, let me suggest another translation of this command to be holy. Here God is saying, Be like me. That's right. God wants you and I to be like him. Holiness is at the essence of who God is.

To be holy means to be full of God in every part of life. The Apostle Peter suggests five things in *1 Peter 1:13-16* we need for our lives to be filled with God. First, as Christians, you are to be actively, *"preparing your minds for action..."* An equivalent expression today would be, "Take off your coat, roll up your sleeves, and get to work." If you want to be holy, you've got to control your mind. God has no use for a believer with a flabby mind. We need to learn to think, think hard, and think things through carefully.

Peter's next instruction is we are to be *"sober minded..."* The underlying Greek word means "wine-less." It speaks of the need to be free from the clouding influence of alcohol or any other narcotic stimulant. Alcohol drags us away from God because it has the propensity to cloud our moral and spiritual judgment. What else could cloud our spiritual or moral judgment? A wrong friendship, a harmful TV show, a bad habit, certain music or certain environments could do it.

Third, we are to *"set your hope fully on the grace that will be brought to you at the revelation of Jesus Christ."* We all set our hope on something. A student sets his hope on graduation, a bride sets her hope on the wedding day, a candidate sets his hope on winning the election. There are many things we set our hope on that controls our lives. However, nothing should be more important than preparing for the day of Jesus returns. Peter says, "You will see Jesus when he returns to the earth. Keep your eyes on the prize."

The fourth thing Peter calls us to do is to be *"obedient children, do not be conformed to the passions of your former ignorance..."* Peter calls his readers to be "obedient children" contrasting it with the way they used to live before they came to Christ. The message is simple: Don't slip back into your old way of life. Peter is talking about your outward life; the part other people can see. That's what the word "conformed" means. Back then you didn't know any better. Now you do. So, watch how you live.

Fifth and lastly, we are to *but as he who called you is holy, you also be holy in all your conduct, ¹⁶ since it is written, "You shall be holy, for I am holy."* This should be the ultimate goal for every Christian. Holiness. We know God and God is holy. Holiness is the essence of what it means to be God. If you are a Christian, there ought to be a family resemblance. As God's children, our desire ought to reflect the character of our heavenly Father to the world.

Today pray your Pastor will stay healthy, whole and holy in every way. Pray your Pastor will understand the call to be holy. Pray your Pastor will be prepared for action, be sober-minded, and set his hope fully on the grace and revelation of Jesus Christ. Pray your Pastor will be as an obedient child, no longer chasing after old passions but his new position and place in Jesus Christ. Pray your Pastor will, through prayer and meditation on the Word of God, begin to look like his heavenly Father and seek to be holy as God is holy.

MY PRAYER:

_____

_____

_____

_____

_____

_____

_____

_____

_____

_____

_____

_____

_____

_____

_____

_____

_____

_____

DAY 29

Read Isaiah 26:3.

Isaiah 26:3 says: *You keep him in perfect peace whose mind is stayed on you, because he trusts in you.* What a wonderful promise. This Scripture was written in the darkest period of Israel's history. So, it may well prove to be a special help to us today when we are surrounded by much gloom and depression and constantly threatened with the three great enemies: doubt, fear and worry.

When all is going well, and the skies are bright, it is easy to read, rehearse and recite, *"You keep him in perfect peace whose mind is stayed on you, because he trusts in you."* But when clouds of trials, disappointment, fear and alarm drift across our sky and the sun is hidden, then how precious these words become to us! There is no promise anywhere in the Bible that encourages us to believe while we are in our earthly bodies we will experience freedom from trouble. There is, however, something far better. There is the promise of peace during the time of trouble. Of what value, would freedom from trouble be if we had no inward peace? Yet how wonderful it is that during the fiercest battle, and while the storm is at its highest, the trusting soul may experience inward peace, a deep-down calm and a quiet confidence!

The writer describes the peace we can experience as "perfect peace". But what is perfect peace? Can we define it? Yes. It is a condition of freedom from disturbance within the soul. It is perfect harmony reigning within. The Hebrew word "shalom" has in it the idea of soundness of health. That means to be filled with perfect peace is to be spiritually healthy and free from all discord within the soul. There can be no room for jealousy, envy, discontent, an uncontrolled temper, selfishness, pride or intolerance in the soul which is filled with peace, for all these things are disturbing factors in the heart. They are discordant notes. The peace which God offers, and which we by His grace may experience, is very practical and perfect.

Now this "perfect peace" is not for everyone. It is for the one: (1) *whose mind is stayed on you*; and (2) *he trusts in you.*" It is for the one who expresses his or her faith both with the head and with the heart. What is the difference? With our head, we believe and with our heart we trust. With our head, we believe God is the Author of peace and the Giver of peace; with our heart, we trust Him to bestow what He promises. Our head and our heart join forces as we read and meditate on God's Word.

Let me share this one last thought with you. Notice Isaiah 26:3 begins with God and ends with God. It begins with "*You*" and it ends with "*you*." There is the first "You" spelled capital Y-o-u and then there is the second "you" spelled lowercase y-o-u. Perfect peace is the Lord Himself within us, not an experience, not a doctrine, an "it," but the Lord Himself. And when we decide to stay in between by faith, then as the great hymn writer, Thomas A. Dorsey, wrote in 1937 we will have "Peace in the Valley." The chorus of this song says, "There'll be peace in the valley for me some way, there'll be peace in the valley for me. I pray no more sorrow and sadness or trouble will be, there'll be peace in the valley for me."

Today, pray your Pastor experiences God's perfect peace with focus and steadfast trust. Pray your Pastor will submit to the strength and sovereignty of God in all things, knowing all things work together for the good of them who love God and are called according to His purpose. Pray your Pastor will be able to endure trials, troubles and temptation. Pray your Pastor will be free from all discord within his soul. Pray your Pastor will possess both peace in his head and in his heart to experience the perfect peace God promised.

MY PRAYER:

_____

_____

_____

_____

_____

_____

_____

_____

_____

_____

_____

_____

_____

_____

_____

_____

_____

DAY 30

Read 1 Peter 3:12.

1 Peter 3:10-11 says: *[10] For Whoever desires to love life and see good days, let him keep his tongue from evil and his lips from speaking deceit; [11] let him turn away from evil and do good; let him seek peace and pursue it.* Wouldn't you like to live a long and happy life? Do you wish for the "good life"? If so, pay attention to what Peter says. These verses describe the life God will bless. If we want the good life: First, keep our tongue from evil. Second, keep our lips from deceitful speech. Third, turn from evil and do good. Fourth, seek peace and pursue it.

When we live like this, we receive the promises of verse 12. *[12] For the eyes of the Lord are on the righteous, and his ears are open to their prayer. But the face of the Lord is against those who do evil. "* God hears our prayers when we do the things outlined in verses 10-11. Think about that for a moment. When we are obedient to His Word the eyes of God are upon us to bless us and his ears are attentive to our prayers. When we give up trying to get even with people, the Lord is free to take vengeance on our enemies any way he sees fit.

As I thought about this passage, it occurred to me for us to live this way, we need a certain view of ourselves, a certain view of God, and a certain view of our enemies. Let me explain. The proper view of ourselves and of God comes from one of my favorite passages found in *Romans 5:6-10:* *⁶ For while we were still weak, at the right time Christ died for the ungodly. ⁷ For one will scarcely die for a righteous person—though perhaps for a good person one would dare even to die— ⁸ but God shows his love for us in that while we were still sinners, Christ died for us. ⁹ Since, therefore, we have now been justified by his blood, much more shall we be saved by him from the wrath of God. ¹⁰ For if while we were enemies we were reconciled to God by the death of his Son, much more, now that we are reconciled, shall we be saved by his life.* Think about the phrase, "while we were enemies." Enemies of who? God's enemy. Is there anything sadder than that under the sun? You and I were once enemies of God. We stood in opposition and opposite sides of the Lord Almighty. We mocked His name, rejected His counsel, resisted His Spirit, blasphemed His Son, and all the while refusing His grace. We were all enemies of God. Not some of us. All of us. By nature, we were born rebels. We came into this world as enemies of the Lord and God in His grace loved us.

While we were ungodly. While we were sinners. While we were powerless. While we were his enemies. He sent his Son to die for us. He gave us His Word. He sent the Holy Spirit to convict us. And one day while we were running away from Him, He found us, brought us to our knees, opened our eyes, gave us new life, caused us to see Jesus, gave us a desire to reach out, pointed us to the cross, and gave us a heart to believe His gospel. And in one shining, amazing, supernatural moment, we were no longer enemies, no longer ungodly, and no longer strangers. Suddenly by grace we became the children of God. He reconciled us to himself in the death of his Son. Enemies became friends. This is the very miracle of the gospel.

If we had a million years and a million lives, we could never pay God back for what He did for us. We could never give enough or sing enough or pray enough or work enough. Our indebtedness and our gratitude will last for eternity. There is, however, one thing we can and we must do. We can do for others what God has done for us.

Today, pray your Pastor's prayers will reach the attentive ears of God as he faces the plots and plans of evil men and women in the church. Pray your Pastor will keep his tongue from evil, keep his lips from deceitful speech, turn from evil and do good, seek peace and pursue it. Pray your Pastor will allow the Lord God to take vengeance on his enemies as He sees fit. Pray your Pastor will be free of envy, malice, anger and hatred toward anyone or anything. Pray your Pastor will view his enemies as God viewed us when we were His enemies and while we were yet sinners He showed us grace, love and forgiveness.

MY PRAYER:

_____

_____

_____

_____

_____

_____

_____

_____

_____

_____

_____

_____

_____

_____

_____

_____

_____

DAY 31

Read Hebrew 13:17.

Church, God has honored you greatly! He has given you a Pastor. He has given you a man of God. He has given you someone who will pray for you, love you, tell you the truth, carry you in his heart, serve you faithfully and who will do so much for you that only in eternity will you know the depth of his commitment.

The writer of Hebrews tells us how we are to respond to the man God has given as Pastor. *Hebrews 13:17a* says: ***Obey your leaders and submit to them, for they are keeping watch over your souls, as those who will have to give an account.*** The Bible is not calling for us to blindly follow the man of God. Before you can follow him, you must look at his walk. This is not a call to criticism or to a judgmental attitude regarding your Pastor. If you look too closely at any man's life you will find many areas of fault and failure. This is a call for the church to watch him as he walks with God by faith. The church needs to observe the convictions that grip his heart. You should understand he carries you in his heart. See the depth of his convictions; the reality of his walk with God; the commitment he demonstrates; the faithfulness that characterizes his life, and the burden he carries for the church and for the Lord. See these things and know he is God's man; he is worthy to be followed; and he is worthy of the respect due. Let his life serve as an example for your own walk with the Lord.

When a servant of God is faithfully following the will of God, teaching and preaching the Word of God, the response of the people of God should be to submit to and be obedient to him. We are living in a time like never before. I remember a time as a young boy when the position of pastor was held in the highest esteem. However, now there is a dismissive and frivolous attitude toward pastoral authority. Honor and respect appears to be a thing of the past. Let me quickly say, I understand there are those that have taken advantage of the office; however, we should still hold to authority of God's Word that commands us who are followers to honor, obey and submit to those who keep watch over our souls.

Hebrews 13:17b further states that obedience to godly church leaders is for your benefit, ***let them do this with joy and not with groaning, for that would be of no advantage to you.*** Disobedience to the man of God "would be of no advantage to you". God designed authority to protect and bless. If you disobey godly church leaders who proclaim God's Word to you, you are truly disobeying God, which always has serious consequences. I remember growing up and one of the things you would look forward to being left in-charge when your parents would leave for a few hours. When that time came in the Gaddis household, my mother or father would say, to all the children left in your charge, now he/she is in charge. We had to obey them as we would have obeyed mom or dad. We obeyed not because we feared the older sibling's punishment we were worried about what my parents would do. And likewise, we are instructed to obey our leaders because it is God's punishment we should be concerned about.

Also see here the Hebrew writer says we are to obey our Pastors ***with joy and not with groaning***. Spiritual children, like our natural children, can be the source of immense joy or of immense grief. Every pastor has experienced obedience from the flock with both joy and groaning. However, the Pastor's true desire is to be like the apostle Paul who told the Thessalonians in *1 Thessalonians 3:9, For what thanksgiving can we return to God for you, for all the joy that we feel for your sake before our God.* The apostle John also wrote in *3 John 1:4, I have no greater joy than to hear that my children are walking in the truth.*

Final word, I am often asked what can I do for my Pastor or how can I pray for my pastor. My answer never changes. I share the very thing I have said to the wonderful people of the Greater Bethel Church, where I have had the privilege to serve for over 25 years as pastor.

First, prepare your heart for church by taking some time during the week, perhaps on Saturday evenings, to pray for your Pastor. Pray that your heart would be open and submissive to God's Word.

Second, pray for those who will be in attendance who are saved and for those who have not yet surrendered to the awesome love of God through Jesus Christ and need to be saved.

Third, pray against distractions that arise.

Fourth, pray for individuals you know of who are struggling with sin.

Fifth, pray your pastor will maintain a good conscience before God and preach His truth without compromise. Pray for your pastor while he is preaching that the seed of the Word would find fertile soil in the hearts of those who are listening.

Let me leave you with this story. On one of his visits to the Continent, Charles Spurgeon met an American minister who said, "I have long wished to see you, Mr. Spurgeon, and to put one or two simple questions to you. In our country, there are many opinions as to the secret of your great influence. Would you be good enough to give me your own point of view?" After a moment's pause, Spurgeon replied, "My people pray for me" (in Iain Murray, *The Forgotten Spurgeon* [Banner of Truth], p. 44). Although every Pastor's gift is different, there is no doubt in my mind that I can speak on behalf of all Pastors and ask that you pray for them. Not just once but consistently, continuously, and compassionately.

Today, pray your Pastor will be able to lead obedient members who are thankful and seek to bring joy and not sorrow to his ministry. Pray your Pastor will walk with God by faith in all things. Pray that your Pastor will seek to please God by being an example to those who are following him. Pray your Pastor will be a servant of God who faithfully follows the will of God, teaching and preaching the Word of God. Pray your Pastor will stand only on the authority of God's Word that commands His followers to honor, obey and submit to those who keep watch over our souls.

MY PRAYER:

_____

_____

_____

_____

_____

_____

_____

_____

_____

_____

_____

_____

_____

_____

_____

_____

SMALL GROUP
LESSONS

2 Timothy 2:15 (ESV)
[15] Do your best to present yourself to God as one approved, a worker who has no need to be ashamed, rightly handling the word of truth.

Hebrews 4:12(ESV)
[12] For the word of God is living and active, sharper than any two-edged sword, piercing to the division of soul and of spirit, of joints and of marrow, and discerning the thoughts and intentions of the heart.

The Bible says, "Therefore, if anyone is in Christ, he is a new creation. The old has passed away; behold, the new has come." The question then is, "What does it mean to be 'in Christ'? It means ultimately that we KNOW Him. It means that we don't just speak about Him, but that we are intimately acquainted with Him. When we know Him, we can experience a personal relationship, a powerful relationship, and a painful relationship with Him. Becoming more like Christ requires pain. It is not an option. There are some impurities inside of you that can only be removed with intense heat. We must spend some time in the crucible of life. When we are comfortable we tend to rely on our own strength. When our life is uncomfortable we tend to rely on God more.

As we walk together the next six weeks through these Bible Study lessons "examine yourself". Take a close look at yourself and be honest about what you believe. It is okay if you have some doubts. Our prayer is that for some a foundation of belief is built and for others your foundation may be strengthened. The goal is to come out of the next seven weeks with no doubt about what we believe. It is important for you to spend your own individual time with each lesson. We have provided for you Bible Study notes to assist you in your private study time. These notes give a more in depth look at the important verses in each chapter for the lesson. More importantly than that you have the Holy Spirit that dwells within you that can give you what you need because of your desire to learn more about it.

POINT TO PONDER

Take a minute to think about what your goal
is for this Spiritual Growth Campaign. Write
down your goal in the space provided below.

_____

_____

_____

_____

_____

_____

_____

_____

Before we begin this study join us in a Prayer of Commitment:

Heavenly Father thank you for another opportunity to learn more about you. Father I admit that I am not all that I need to be for You; however, I do desire to be better. Help me to honor my commitment to this Bible Study. To commit not only to public study time but also private study time preparing for each week's lesson. Help me to be aware of the distractions that Satan will send to pull me off the path and to put on the whole armor of God that I may be able to stand continuously. I commit to praying daily for the facilitator of this class and also each and every person who has chosen to walk with me through this journey. In Jesus' precious name I pray Amen.

OPENING PRAYER

Father, I draw near to you now with hunger and expectation, with joy and delight. I love being fed by You, Lord. I am hungry. I want to feed on the Word of God, the Bread of Life. And I thank You, Lord, for the Holy Spirit. I am thirsty for you so Lord Jesus, I come to You believing that You can meet this need, quench this thirst, and fill me with Your Spirit as You teach and enlighten me. I ask You to give me understanding to guide me into all the truth. And I am asking, Lord, for more than just comprehension, but for an apprehension and appropriation of believing and walking in the very things that You speak to me about. I ask that the very Word that was breathed out by You will have its perfect work that I may be mature, not lacking anything. I ask that your will be done during my time of studying Your Word, in Jesus' name. Amen.

WINNING IN YOUR QUIET TIME
WEEK ONE

"God's best for you is closely linked with this daily meeting with Him. The barometer of one's Christian life is the Quiet Time. Do you have a Quiet Time, or have you let it slip? Be the man of God who takes time to be holy, speaks oft with his Lord, abides in Him only, and feeds on His Word. God grant that this may be true of you. You cannot tell me you have surrendered to God, that Jesus Christ is Lord of your life, or that you know the fullness of the Holy Spirit unless you have your manna in the morning. May your prayer be: Help me, O Lord, Thy Word to read, Upon the living Bread to feed, Seeking Thy Spirit's quickening lead that I may please Thee in all things." ~Stephen F. Olford

PAUSE AND PONDER

Discuss ways that Christians grow in Christ daily as a Christian?

PERSONAL STUDY

Mark 1:35 says *"And rising very early in the morning, while it was still dark, he departed and went out to a desolate place, and there he prayed."* **Luke 5:16 says** *"But he would withdraw to desolate places and pray."* We are not told where this "desolated or solitary" place was, because we are not told, however the importance is that He had a place where He could be alone with God. Jesus needed to be along with God. If Jesus, the Son of Man, valued alone time with God to seek His will, His way and His Word, how much more must we?

Today, we are going to learn how to win in our quite time. A daily quiet time is a private meeting each day between a disciple and the Lord Jesus Christ. It should not be impromptu. We should commune with the Lord on a spur-of-the-moment basis many times each day, but a quiet time is a period we set aside in advance for the sole purpose of personal meeting with our Savior and Lord.

Five reasons we should spend quiet time with God:

1. A quiet time allows us to know God and His ways. The Bible is God's Word given to us. It is His revelation of Himself. As we study God's Word, we learn His ways, His nature and character. (Psalm 119:15; Psalm 119:33; Psalm 119:37)

2. A quiet time allows us to keep our way pure. As we focus our attention on God and meditate on His Word, we gradually look less like the world and more like Christ. (Psalm 119:9-11; Psalm 119:105; James 4:8)

3. A quiet time allows us to keep our mind renewed. As we spend time with God and understand the Scriptures, the lies of the world, the flesh and the devil are exposed, and the Truth of God is illuminated. By saturating our minds with the Truth, our minds are renewed and transformed. (Romans 12:1-2; Matthew 22:37)

4. A quiet time allows us to keep our spiritual roots firmly planted. When are lives our rooted in God's Word, we are like trees grounded in His love. (Psalm 1:1-

5) Knowing God and His Truth will enable us to ward off spiritual attack and resist believing the lies of the enemy. (Ephesians 6:10-20)

5. A quiet time allows us to stay strong enough to refute and refuse false teaching. Christians are often bombarded with teaching that distorts God's Truth and misrepresents His character. By spending time with Him and reading His Word, you will be able to stand up against such false teachings. (Ephesians 4:14; Hebrews 13:9)

GROUP STUDY

Introduction

What elements are vital to a strong and sustainable quite time?

Read: Luke 10:38-42

Observation

What did Martha do for Jesus and those that were traveling with Him? (vv. 38)

Where was Mary during all of this? (vv. 39)

What was Mary doing while Martha attended to their guest? (vv. 39-40)

What caused Martha to become "distracted (ESV) or cumbered (KJV)"? (vv. 40) *The word "cumbered" (periespato) means to draw around, to twist, to be drawn here and there, to be distracted.*

What did Martha accuse her sister Mary of and Jesus of? (vv. 40)

What did Jesus make of the choices of both sister? (vv. 41-42)

Interpretation

Do you spend time with God daily? What does it look like?

Application

How can your quiet times with God be improved? What are the next steps to ensure these changes are made?

DEEPER STUDY

Introduction

How would having a dedicated and deeper quite time with God change your entire life?

Read: Philippians 4: 4-9

Observation

What did Paul encourage his readers to do? (v.4)

How did Paul tell the Philippian Christians to treat others? (v.5)

What did Paul say about anxiety? (vv. 6-7)

What were the Philippians to do instead of worrying? (vv.6-7)

How can a believer enjoy the peace of God? (vv. 6-7)

What are the qualities of wholesome thoughts? (v.8)

What were the Philippians to put into practice? (v.9)

How can believers enjoy the presence of the God of peace? (v.9)

Interpretation

How can you have a peaceful spirit?

What does it take for you to think worthy thoughts?

Application

What can you do today to reduce your level of anxiety?

A winning strategy for
Quiet Time with God:

Pick a **Place**...The quieter the better! *[A patio area, kitchen table, desk, park, library]*

Pick a **Period**...When you are most refreshed! *[Early morning, lunchtime, break time, bed time]*

Pick a **Prayer**...Or two or three! *[Thanking, praising, asking, confessing, admitting, requesting God]*

Pick a **Passage**... *[A Psalm, parable, proverb, epistle, story, section]*

Pick a **Project**... *[Journaling, singing, writing, reading devotional, charting, meditating, memorizing]*

WINNING IN YOUR PRAYER LIFE
WEEK 2

"The Church is looking for better methods; God is looking for better men." "What the Church needs to-day is not more machinery or better, not new organizations or more and novel methods, but men whom the Holy Ghost can use -- men of prayer, men mighty in prayer. ~ **E.M. Bounds**

PAUSE AND PONDER

What thoughts come to mind when you hear the word "prayer"?

PERSONAL STUDY

Prayer is one of the most powerful things a Child of God can do. Talking to God, whether by thought or tongue, is the greatest of all privileges that you and I have been given. Prayer allows us, as believers to commune and converse with God. Prayer affords us to fellowship with God and is the one thing God desires most is fellowship with mankind.

Thinking about prayer as the ability to be able to go directly into the presence of the Lord is an honor beyond description, **Hebrews 4:16** says, *Let us then with confidence draw near to the throne of grace, that we may receive mercy and find grace to help in time of need.* To be able to speak to the God Who is Creator and Controller of the entire universe, and to know that He has promised to hear us and to answer us, **Jeremiah 33:3** *Call to me and I will answer you, and will tell you great and hidden things that you have not known.*; **Isaiah 65:24** *Before they call I will answer; while they are yet speaking I will hear*, is a blessing to great to comprehend.

Furthermore, I think it is imperative that we understand and consider the fact that real prayer is not just us sending words out into thin air, but real prayer is used by God to accomplish His purposes on the earth, it boggles the mind! What a gift we have been given! What a privilege is ours, to be able to speak to God; knowing He will hear and He will answer; knowing that He has invited us to be involved with Him in the work He is doing!

But, like anything else in life, we humans can even mess up something as profound and beautiful as prayer. Since the time of Seth in **Genesis 4:26**, men have been calling upon the name of the Lord. Many have prayed properly and have seen God move in tremendous power as He heard and answered those prayers. Others have prayed out of wrong motives and have received nothing in answer to their requests.

There are four major areas we should address when we pray to the Lord:

- **Preeminence.** God, you are majestic and powerful. I yield my life to you.
- **Provision.** Lord, give me your guidance in decision-making.
- **Pardon.** Forgive me for my sins (be specific).
- **Protection.** Keep me from giving in to the temptations of the world.

Our praying can be defined as an activity that must include FACTS. That is an acrostic that is rendered:

- **F – Faith** – Without which we can expect nothing from God (Hebrew 11:1; Matthew 21:22; Mark 11:24)
- **A - Adoration** - God must be worshipped (Psalm 145:1-3; Luke 11:2ff)
- **C - Confession** - Our sin must be dealt with (2 Samuel 12:7ff; Psalm 51:1-5)
- **T - Thanksgiving** - We must always possess a thankful heart before Him. (Ephesians 5:20)
- **S - Supplication** - There is room to tell Him what we need. (Luke 11:9)

GROUP STUDY

Introduction

What images or thoughts spring to mind when you hear the word "prayer"?

Read: Matthew 6:5-15

Observation

What wrong motive does Jesus bring light to in prayer? (v. 5)

What condemnation does Jesus speak toward those who pray for public praise and why? (v. 5)

How did Jesus command His followers to pray? (v. 6)

What did Jesus have to say about repetitive or long, windy prayers? (vv. 7)

What insights or facts about God are revealed in this passage? (vv. 6; 8; 9)

To whom did Jesus tell us to pray? (v.9)

What should be our attitude toward God? (v.9)

What should be our attitude toward God's kingdom and will? (v.10)

What should be our attitude toward life's necessities? (v.11)

What should be our attitude toward those who have wronged us? (v.12)

What should be our attitude toward temptation? (v.13)

Why is it crucial for us to forgive those who wrong us? (vv.14-15)

Interpretation

If God knows what we need before we ask, why should we pray?

If Jesus commands us to pray in secret, what is the value of public prayer?

Why do many Christians feel uncomfortable praying out loud?

Application

Make a list of the challenges you currently have in your prayer life. Now list the changes you plan to implement in your prayer life today. Be sure to add them to your prayer list.

DEEPER STUDY

Introduction:

Write down a name of someone that challenges you to be a better Christian. What about them challenges you to be better?

Read: Luke 18:9-14

Observation

Who were the two men described in the story? (vv.10)

What did the Pharisee do? (vv.11)

What motivated the Pharisee to pray? (vv.11)

How did the Pharisee pray? (vv.11-12)

Why did the tax collector stand at a distance? (vv.13)

What does the tax collector's posture reveal about his own attitude? (vv.13)

What difference did it make how these men prayed? (vv.14)
What principle did Jesus stress? (vv.14)

Interpretation

How do you approach God in your prayers?

What does this parable teach us about our prayer habits?

Application

What specific steps can you make this week to strengthen your prayer life?

WINNING IN YOUR BIBLE STUDY
WEEK 3

"There are times when solitude is better than society, and silence is wiser than speech. We should be better Christians if we were more alone, waiting upon God, and gathering through meditation on His Word spiritual strength for labour in his service. We ought to muse upon the things of God, because we thus get the real nutriment out of them. . .. Why is it that some Christians, although they hear many sermons, make but slow advances in the divine life? Because they neglect their closets, and do not thoughtfully meditate on God's Word. They love the wheat, but they do not grind it; they would have the corn, but they will not go forth into the fields to gather it; the fruit hangs upon the tree, but they will not pluck it; the water flows at their feet, but they will not stoop to drink it. From such folly deliver us, O Lord. . .." ~ **Charles H. Spurgeon**

PAUSE AND PONDER

Imagine that you are a reporter for a local newspaper or radio station and was asked to gather information to report on a very important cover story. What six questions (hint) would you ask to gather information to write and report a good factual story?

PERSONAL STUDY

We cannot properly honor and serve God unless we have knowledge of His will, *Romans 12:2* records, *"Do not be conformed to this world, but be transformed by the renewal of your mind, that by testing you may discern what is the will of God, what is good and acceptable and perfect."* *Colossians 4:12* says, *"...that you may stand mature and fully assured in all the will of God."* *Hebrews 10:36* clearly states the importance of personal Bible study like this, *"For you have need of endurance, so that when you have done the will of God you may receive what is promised."* The knowledge we need to win is gleamed from spending time in regular, diligent Bible study.

In *Luke 2:52* we learn a valuable lesson on growing, "And Jesus increased in wisdom and in stature and in favor with God and man." Jesus explains the developmental process in His life: "Jesus grew..." we are told in four areas:

- He grew "in wisdom" – *intellectual development*
- He grew "in stature" – *physical development*
- He grew "in favor with God" – *spiritual development*
- And He grew "in favor with men" – *social and emotional development*

Here are three important lesson about why studying the Bible is vital:

1. Bible Study is vital because through it we can know God's Will. Paul says in *2 Timothy 3:16-17* *"All Scripture is breathed out by God and profitable for teaching, for reproof, for correction, and for training in righteousness, that the man of God may be complete, equipped for every good work."* What makes Bible Study so necessary is found in **Romans 10:17** *"faith comes from hearing, and hearing through the word of Christ."* In order words Scriptures are necessary to our salvation. ***John 3:16-17*** *"For God so loved the world, that he gave his only Son, that whoever believes in him should not perish but have eternal life. For God did not send his Son into the world to condemn the world, but in order that the world might be saved through him.*

2. Bible Study is vital because through it we can know <u>God's Word</u>. When we carefully read, and reflect on His Word our attitude toward God Word changes. ***Psalm 119:97-104*** shares this, *97 Oh how I love your law! It is my meditation all the day. 98 Your commandment makes me wiser than my enemies, for it is ever with me. 99 I have more understanding than all my teachers, for your testimonies are my meditation. 100 I understand more than the aged, for I keep your precepts. 101 I hold back my feet from every evil way, in order to keep your word. 102 I do not turn aside from your rules, for you have taught me. 103 How sweet are your words to my taste, sweeter than honey to my mouth! 104 Through your precepts I get* *understanding; therefore I hate every false way.*

3. Bible Study is vital because through it we can know <u>God's Way</u>. Growing spiritually through meaningful personal and corporate Bible study is summed up by Paul in **Philippians 1:9-11** *"And it is my prayer that your love may abound more and more, with knowledge and all discernment, ¹⁰ so that you may approve what is excellent, and so be pure and blameless for the day of Christ, filled with the fruit of righteousness that comes through Jesus Christ, to the glory and praise of God."* Notice the sharp criticism of some who had not taken the time to accurately discern God's way from diligent study of His word. **Hebrews 5:12-14** shares this thought, *"For though by this time you ought to be teachers, you need someone to teach you again the basic principles of the oracles of God. You need milk, not solid food, for everyone who lives on milk is unskilled in the word of righteousness, since he is a child. But solid food is for the mature, for those who have their powers of discernment trained by constant practice to distinguish good from evil."*

GROUP STUDY

Introduction: How important is milk to a baby and food to an adult? How does that relate to studying the Bible?

Read: 2 Timothy 3:14-17

Observation

What did Paul encourage Timothy to do? (vv.14)

How long had Timothy known the holy Scriptures? (vv.15)

What are the holy Scriptures able to do? (vv.15)

What is true of all Scripture? (vv.16)

For what is Scripture useful? (vv.16)

For what good work does the Scripture equip the person of God? (vv.17)

Interpretation
What does it mean that the Bible is God-breathed?

How equipped are you to do every good work?

What type of doctrines do people today like to hear?

How are scriptures useful in the following ways?
- **Teaching:** Deut. 6:4-9
- **Rebuking**: Hebrews 4:12-13
- **Correcting**: Psalm 19:7-11
- **Training in Righteousness**: Psalm 119:25-32

Application

List different ways you can use the Bible in your own spiritual growth this week.

DEEPER STUDY

Introduction

What are some reasons a relationship would begin to deteriorate? What would help the relationship get better?

Read: Psalm 119:1-16

Observation

Who will be blessed by God? (vv.1-3)

What are we to do with God's commands? (vv.4)

What is the personal effect when a believer does not keep His Word? (vv.6)

How do we properly apply God's Word according to the psalmist? (vv.7)

What is the potential result of a lack of obedience to His Word? (vv.8)

What is the main issue raised in the next verse? (vv.9)

What does it mean to seek God with your whole heart? (vv.10)

What do each of the words below mean to you personally if correctly done? (vv.9-13)
- *"Keeping"* (v.9)

- *"Seek"* (v.10)

- "S*tored up"'* (v.11)

- "I have declared" (v.13)

What do each of the phrases below mean to you? (vv.14-16)

- *"...I delight in...Your testimonies"* (v.14)

- *"...meditate on Your precepts"* (v.15)

- *"...fix my eyes on Your ways"* (v.15)

- "...delight in Your statutes" (v.16)

- *"...not forget Your word"* (v.16)

Interpretation

What role should God's Word play in our lives?

How should we read and study God's Word?

How can we show our respect for God's written Word?

Application

How could you improve the quality or quantity of the time you spend reading and meditating on God's Word this week?

In what specific ways could you demonstrate your love for God's word in the next few weeks?

WINNING IN YOUR WORSHIP LIFE
WEEK FOUR

"When you consider all of the words used for worship in both the Old and New Testaments, and when you put the meanings together, you find that worship involves both attitudes (awe, reverence, respect) and actions (bowing, praising, serving). It is both a subjective experience and an objective activity. Worship is not an unexpressed feeling, nor is it an empty formality. True worship is balanced and involves the mind, the emotions, and the will. It must be intelligent; it must reach deep within and be motivated by love; and it must lead to obedient actions that glorify God." ~ **Warren Wiersbe**

PAUSE AND PONDER

What ingredients come to mind when you think of worship other than singing?

PERSONAL STUDY

I wish I could transport you back in time to the early church, so you could attend 45 minutes or so of a worship service. The experience would change you forever.

As you observed the believers devoting themselves to the apostles' teaching, to fellowship, to the breaking of bread, to prayer, and to praising God (**Acts 2:42–47**), I believe you would say, "Wow, listen to how they speak to God! He seems so real to them! They seem to have such intimacy, such freedom, and such power!"

In those few minutes, you would witness worship in the early church, and you would see how the Holy Spirit manifested the intimacy and awesomeness of God's presence to the believers as they praised and worshipped Him. Then, I think you would say, "I wish I could experience that too!"

I believe you can. But before you can experience the benefits of worship, you must understand what worship is, why worship is important, and what happens when you worship.

What is worship? Worship without truth does nothing for us and God rejects worship that is not done in truth. Truth without the Spirit is a manmade worship so true worship must be in the Spirit and in truth. God is seeking those who will worship Him in this manner. The hour has now come.

By definition, worship is ascribing worth to something or someone. But true worship is also a matter of the heart. It must be felt. It can't be ritualistic. It can't be just an external act, going through the motions.

True worship is a heartfelt expression of love, adoration, admiration, fascination, wonder, and celebration. It's something that happens in your heart and soul when you begin to praise God for who He is and thank Him for what He has done.

There is nothing difficult about worship. Christian or non-Christian, pagan or holy, every human being was designed to worship, and does worship—something. Consider a group of sports fans watching and talking about a game. They worship. Consider a group of teenagers at a concert. They worship.

We worship food, sports, arts, and music. We worship comfort, control, power, achievement, work, money, and relationships; but, God calls us to worship Him. He commands and desires it, He pursues it, He deserves it, and He will reward it. For God bestows His provision, grace, sovereignty, and power on those who worship Him in spirit and in truth.

But if you choose not to worship God, you need to understand that you are worshipping something else. And whether you worship a job, achievement, money, or a person, you are doing so to your detriment. At some point, the object of your worship will fail to come through for you.

Perhaps the best way to illustrate what happens when we worship is to look at the worship experience of one of God's prophets recorded in *Isaiah 6:1-8:*

1. Genuine and authentic worship is seen in our new upward gaze. Isaiah writes *[1] In the year that King Uzziah died I saw the Lord sitting upon a throne, high and lifted up; and the train of his robe filled the temple. [2] Above him stood the seraphim. Each had six wings:*

with two he covered his face, and with two he covered his feet, and with two he flew. ³ And one called to another and said: "Holy, holy, holy is the LORD of hosts; the whole earth is full of his glory!" ⁴ And the foundations of the thresholds shook at the voice of him who called, and the house was filled with smoke. Isaiah glance at God on His throne in all His glory. It refocuses our view of God. It pulls our affections off our idols and puts them onto God. It causes us to remember how good He is, how big, kind, powerful, and loving He is, and how holy He is.

2. Genuine and authentic worship is seen in our new inward gaze. Isaiah continues painting us a picture of worship in verses, *⁵ And I said: "Woe is me! For I am lost; for I am a man of unclean lips, and I dwell in the midst of a people of unclean lips; for my eyes have seen the King, the LORD of hosts!" ⁶ Then one of the seraphim flew to me, having in his hand a burning coal that he had taken with tongs from the altar. ⁷ And he touched my mouth and said: "Behold, this has touched your lips; your guilt is taken away, and your sin atoned for."* When you see God for who He really is, as Isaiah did, you start to see yourself for who you really are. You start seeing things in your heart and in your life that really didn't bother you before. But notice that after Isaiah saw and confessed his sinfulness, he also experienced the mercy, grace, and forgiveness of God. That's what happens when you really worship.

3. Genuine and authentic worship is seen in our new outward gaze. Isaiah's upward gaze, produced an inward gaze that ultimately lead to a new outward gaze. Notice that Isaiah's inward look is followed by an outward look.

[8] And I heard the voice of the Lord saying, "Whom shall I send, and who will go for us?" Then I said, "Here I am! Send me." Genuine worship always leads to an outward look—a personal response or action—a desire to be obedient to whatever God calls you to do.

Genuine worship isn't just singing songs and getting a good feeling in your heart. Genuine worship is seeing God for who He really is— His power, His greatness, His holiness, His sovereignty, His love, and His compassion— and then giving Him what He's worth—the best of your time, your talents, your thoughts, your words, and your deeds.

True worship is seeing afresh the tremendous worth of God and, in response, giving Him the best of everything you have.

GROUP STUDY

Introduction

When you hear the word "Worship" what images and thoughts come to mind in defining what real "Worship" is in your life?

Read: **Romans 12:1-8**

Observation

How do people properly worship God? (v.1)

What is the most reasonable response to God's great mercy? (vv.1-2)

How is the Christian to be different from unbelieving people? (v.2)

How should the mind of a Christian be changed? (v.2)

What must happen in order for a person to discern and agree with the will of God? (v.2)

How should Christians think about themselves? (v.3)

What makes Christians different from one another? (vv.4-6)

What did Paul use the human body to illustrate? (vv.4-5)

What are the gifts of God and how should each person use their gift? (vv.6-8)

Interpretation

What right does God have to ask us for a full-life commitment to Him?

What makes offering our bodies as living sacrifices an act of worship?

What are the patterns of the world that tempt us to conform?

What gifts from God do you see in others?

What gifts from God do you see in your life?

Application

How can you put a spiritual gift to work as an act of worship for others this week?

DEEPER STUDY

Introduction

What new principal have you learned about worshipping God through this study?

Read: Psalm 95:1-11

Observation

How is the Lord described? (vv.1, 3, 6)

What call did the psalm writer give to God's people? (vv.1-5)

What reasons did the psalm writer give Israel to praise the Lord? (vv. 3-5)

How did the psalm writer advise the righteous to demonstrate their submission to God? (v.6)

What should motivate God's people to worship Him? (vv.6-7)

What advice did this psalm offer to the Israelites? (vv.6-11)

How did the psalm writer want Israel to respond differently to God's voice? (vv.7-11)

Why did the psalm writer remind Israel of her rebellion in the past? (vv.8-11)

Why did the Lord expect the Israelites to remain faithful to Him? (v.9)

Why did God condemn Israel to forty years in the desert? (v.10)

What were the consequences of the Israelites' rebellion? (v. 11)

Interpretation

What specific instructions does this psalm give us about worship?

Why do you think the psalmist called God's people to bow before the Lord?

What motivates you to offer praise and thanksgiving to God?

Application

What do you plan to do considering what the psalmist has taught about worship?

How can you become more receptive to God's voice during your private study and corporate preaching?

WINNING IN YOUR CHURCH LIFE
WEEK 5

"Aloneness can lead to loneliness. God's preventative for loneliness is intimacy - meaningful, open, sharing relationships with one another. In Christ we have the capacity for the fulfilling sense of belonging which comes from intimate fellowship with God and with other believers." ~ **Neil T. Anderson**

PAUSE AND PONDER

What things has the devil used to destroy Christian fellowship (koinonia) from being common place in your personal life and in your church life?

PERSONAL STUDY

In the book of Genesis, we are told about how creation and community was first born and why. When God first formed Adam from the dust, he was the only person on the planet. Can you imagine how lonely he must have felt? But it didn't last long. **Genesis 2:18** reads, *"Then the LORD God said, "It is not good that the man should be alone; I will make him a helper fit for him."* Thus, God give Adam some company and He created Eve.

Now nearly eight (8) billion people later, people are everywhere! However, people are lonelier than ever before. Even we might mingle between worship time or catch up around the water cooler at work, but that probably isn't real, authentic community.

As we look at winning in our church life: Let me quickly say as we've already learned in winning in our prayer life, how important it is to spend time alone with God, soaking up His Word. But He does not intend for us to live in total isolation. He specifically designed us to crave and thrive in relationship with others. We are our best selves when we are experiencing life's highs and lows with other believers. **That means everyone, whether you are single or married, needs community.**

The **Bible** has a lot to say about this topic! Here are four reasons the Bible says community is so great.

1. Being in community with other believers is encouraging. Being in community with other believers gives you the chance to be around people at different stages of their faith journey—and to bear their burdens alongside of them **Galatians 6:2** *"Bear one another's burdens, and so fulfill the law of Christ."* That's awesome, because everyone has something to teach and to learn.

2. Being in community with other believers is exciting. Community should never feel dull, forced or fake. In fact, it should be the exact opposite. **Psalm 133:1** teaches us, *"Behold, how good and pleasant it is when brothers dwell in unity!"* As believers we should be the most enthusiasm, exciting, encouraging and enjoyable people on the planet to be around.

3. Being in community with other believers is enticing. The Bible says the Holy Spirit is present whenever believers gather together. A great example of this was the early church of Acts, which made a habit of meeting together, eating together, and worshiping together. **Acts 2:46-47** teaches us, *"And day by day, attending the temple together and breaking bread in their homes, they received* *their food with glad and generous hearts, praising God and having favor with all the people. And the Lord added to their number day by day those who were being saved.*" Being in church on Sundays is definitely important. But if you want to be a Christ follower, be one every day in the context of *all* your communities. *That's* where you'll see ministry happen.

4. Being in community with other believers encourages love. We have all been to a wedding where the Pastor recited the familiar words of **1 Corinthians 13:13** *"So now faith, hope, and love abide, these three; but the greatest of these is love."* Paul held love above *all else* in his letter to the Corinthians. And he did the same with his letter to the Colossians: *[13] bearing with one another and, if one has a complaint against another, forgiving each other; as the Lord has forgiven you, so you also must forgive. [14] And above all these put on love, which binds everything together in perfect harmony.*

5. Being in community with other believers establishes faith. — and is essential to following Christ. **Romans 12:4-5** teaches us, *"For as in one body we have many members,* *and the members do not all have the same function, so we, though many, are one body in Christ, and individually members one of another."* One of the things I love to say is "we are better together than we ever could be alone."

Let me be transparent for just a moment. I understand how hard it is for some of us to commit to community. We have been broken, bruised, beaten and battered by people not from without but from within. Our confidence has been shattered. Our friendship and fellowship has been taken for granted. Our kindness has been viewed and held against us like weakness. Many of us have shut the door of our heart, vowing to live in total isolation and solitude simply to protect what pieces of our heart we still have. Let me say quickly, you cannot allow the devil to win because God has some special blessing in community for you. Sometimes we must laugh in the devil's face and when we grow in our relationships with others, we're growing in relationship with Him!

GROUP STUDY

Introduction

Take a moment to think about your clothes closet. Are there some items you use to wear that you cannot fit or have become out-of-style? Why have you not gotten rid of them?

Read: Colossians 3:1-17

Observation

Where did Paul tell the Colossians to turn their attention? (v.1)

Where did Paul tell the believers to focus their concern? (v.2)

What was the Colossians' security? (v.3)

Why should believers look forward to Christ's return? (v.4)

What must die? (v.5)

1. _____

2. _____

3. _____

4. _____

5. _____

What did the Colossians need to also take off? (vv.7-9)

1. _____

2. _____

3. _____

4. _____

5. _____

6. _____

What virtues does God seek to plant in us? (v.14)

How were the Colossian believers called to clothe themselves?

List the attitudes and actions that help us avoid and resolve conflict. (vv.12-17)

1. _____

2. _____

3. _____

4. _____

5. _____

6. _____

7. _____

Why did Paul call on the believers to be peaceful and thankful? (vv.15-16)

What should we do? How? (v.17)

What is one principle that ought to guide everything we do? (v.17)

Interpretation

What old, "earthly" clothing do you need to get rid of?

How does wearing "Christ's clothing" affect the way you live your daily life?

Application

Which of God's goals for holy living do you need to apply to your life this week?

DEEPER STUDY

Introduction

What functions in the church do you feel are most important? Why?

Read: 1 Corinthians 12:12-26

Observation

In what way are Christians like a human body? (12:12-13)

What makes Christians unified and dependent on one another? (12:13)

What lessons are there in seeing the church as a human body? (12:14-17)

Who arranged the parts of the body of Christ? (12:18)

Why should members of the body of Christ not say to each other, "I don't need you"? (12:21-22)

Why should the less honorable parts be treated with special attention? (12:23)

How has God combined the members of the body of Christ? (12:24-26)

Interpretation

How well do you interact with other members in the body of Christ?

What has God appointed you to be in the body of Christ?

Why do people often assume that certain duties in the church are more important?

Application:

What would be the best way to use your unique abilities in the body of Christ this year?

WINNING IN YOUR STEWARDSHIP LIFE
WEEK 6

"If God was the owner, I was the manager. I needed to adopt a steward's mentality toward the assets He had entrusted - not given - to me. A steward manages assets for the owner's benefit. The steward carries no sense of entitlement to the assets he manages. It's his job to find out what the owner wants done with his assets, then carry out his will."
~ **Randy Alcorn**

PAUSE AND PONDER

Stewardship is as much about ___*living*___ as it is about ___*giving*___. Do you agree or disagree? Why?

PERSONAL STUDY

Read: 2 Corinthians 8:1-5

Among the early churches, it was the Macedonian church (comprised of the churches in Philippi, Berea and Thessalonica) that was well known in the area of giving. Though poor, they were generous in their giving and contributed with great cheerfulness and liberality. In his second epistle to the Corinthians (in chapter 8), the Apostle Paul was trying to encourage the brethren to contribute and give liberally for the relief of the poor brethren in Jerusalem, citing the good examples set by the churches of Macedonia. Walk with me as we look and learn about their generosity:

1. They joyfully and generously gave despite their being poor. The Apostle Paul described the Macedonian churches in **2 Corinthians 8:1-2;** *"We want you to know, brothers, about the grace of God that has been given among the churches of Macedonia, ² for in a severe test of affliction, their abundance of joy and their extreme poverty have overflowed in a wealth of generosity on their part.* Even when they themselves were amid great difficulties and deep poverty, their joy abounded to move them to give generously. They did not allow circumstances to hinder them from giving.

2. They willingly gave as much as they were able. 2 Corinthians 8:3, *"For they gave according to their means, as I can testify, and beyond their means, of their own accord..."* The churches in Macedonia acted spontaneously and did not wait to be urged and pressed to give. Paul testified that they gave beyond what could have been expected from them or beyond what would have been thought possible in their condition.

3. They were determined to give to help meet the needs of others. 2 Corinthians 8:4, *"begging us earnestly for the favor of taking part in the relief of the saints..."* They insisted that Paul should receive their contribution and pass it on to the poor and needy brethren in Jerusalem. They have strong interest and intense desire to relieve the needs of others!

4. They first gave their own selves to the Lord. 2 Corinthians 8:5, *"and this, not as we expected, but they gave themselves first to the Lord and then by the will of God to us."* Their generosity is founded in true piety and on right priority. They first yielded their own selves to the Lord – an act of total surrender of one's life and one's possession to God. Only after they had given themselves unto the Lord, that they gave themselves unto men according to the will of God.

5. They generously gave to support the work of the Lord. Philippians 4:10; 15-16 *¹⁰ I rejoiced in the Lord greatly that now at length you have revived your concern for me. You were indeed concerned for me, but you had no opportunity. ¹⁵ And you Philippians yourselves know that in the beginning of the gospel, when I left Macedonia, no church entered into partnership with me in giving and receiving, except you only. ¹⁶ Even in Thessalonica you sent me help for my needs once and again.*

Of all the churches in Macedonia, it seems that the church at Philippi was the most distinguished for its generosity. Paul commended them for their care and concern which obviously included their commitment to support him in the Gospel work, as he mentioned in Philippians 4:18 of **Philippians 4:18** *I have received full payment, and more. I am well supplied, having received from*

Epaphroditus the gifts you sent, a fragrant offering, a sacrifice acceptable and pleasing to God.

Generosity knows no boundaries. They generously gave to the poor brethren in Jerusalem and went out of their way to send Epaphroditus to bring their gift to Paul who was then inside the cold prison in Rome. Realize that one's generosity to support the Lord's work goes beyond the ministries of the local church to missions allowing great things to be accomplished for the glory of God.

Learning of the generosity of the early church, it would be well to examine ourselves. Have we been generous in our giving? Consider what Paul said in **2 Corinthians 8:7,** *But as you excel in everything—in faith, in speech, in knowledge, in all earnestness, and in our love for you—see that you excel in this act of grace also.* Like the church in general, we should devote ourselves in doctrine, fellowship, breaking of bread and prayers but is found wanting in the grace of giving. May we abound in this grace too! Remember, God loves a cheerful giver!

GROUP STUDY

Introduction

What would you do for God if you knew you could not fail?

Read: Matthew 25:14-30

Observation

What did the man in the parable give to his servants? (v.15)

How did the master react to the report of the first servant? (vv.20-21)

What was the response to the report of the second servant? (vv.22-23)

What excuse did the third servant give for not investing his talent? (vv.24-25)

How did the master respond to the third servant's explanation? (vv.26-27)

What orders did the master give about the third servant's one talent? (vv.28-29)

What judgment was handed down to the "wicked, lazy" servant? (v.30)

Interpretation

With what talents or resources has God entrusted you?

What thoughts or attitudes cause us to be lazy in carrying out our Christian responsibilities?

Application

List ways you will hold yourself more accountable in stewardship?

DEEPER STUDY

Introduction

What images come to your mind when you hear about a "cheerful giver"?

Read 2 Corinthians 9:6-15

Observation

How should we give? Why? (v.7)

What promise does God give to believers who do give generously? (v.8)

What does God provide? (v.10)

What results from the generosity of
Christians? (v.11)

Interpretation

What could a reluctant giver do to become a
more cheerful giver?

Application:

How can you remind yourself of God's
generosity the next time you are tempted to
hold back from giving cheerfully?

Reverend Teron V. Gaddis is the Senior Pastor-Teacher of the Greater Bethel Baptist Church in Oklahoma City, Oklahoma. Pastor Gaddis is one of today's most gifted communicators who offers a clear, contemporary and creative teaching style. He has a passion for making the complex simple as he speaks truth to people in ways they can understand and apply to their everyday lives.

Pastor G's preaching style includes careful exposition of Scripture, combined with his signature detailed stories from contemporary life that enrich the sermon and encourages the congregation.

Pastor G is passionate about changed lives, whether a person is coming to Christ for the very first time or rededicating their life for the 100th time, nothing excites him more than to see people began to live fully committed and capable followers of Jesus Christ. His goal in ministry is to please his heavenly Father and to be a faithful steward of the lives that have been entrusted into his hands.

Pastor G has been married to Janice for thirty-one years and the two of them have five children and ten grandchildren.

After 34 years in ministry and 25 years of pastoring, Pastor G continues to be a leading voice in innovation, inspiration and influence

Small Group Bible Studies
Written by Pastor Teron V. Gaddis
(All studies available for reproduction.
Send request to chiefofstaff@pastorgministries.com)

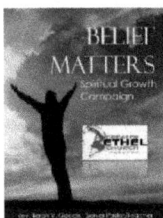

My Belief Matters

An eight-week study on basic Baptist
doctrine with sermon outlines and weekly
Bible Study lessons.

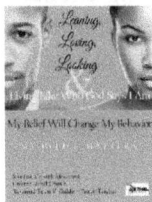

My Belief Will Dictate My Behavior

A ten-week study on the life-changing
power of the Word of God and how your
belief will change your behavior.
Includes Sunday sermon outlines,
Wednesday Bible study outlines and small
group lessons

From Possession to Possession
21 Day Fast
A daily study of the book of Joshua
designed to be incorporated with a time of
prayer and fasting.

www.ingramcontent.com/pod-product-compliance
Lightning Source LLC
Chambersburg PA
CBHW051822090426
42736CB00011B/1614